Narratives of Enterprise

Narratives of Enterprise

Crafting Entrepreneurial Self-Identity in a Small Firm

Simon Down

University of Newcastle upon Tyne Business School, UK

Edward Elgar

Cheltenham, UK • Northampton, MA, USA

Published by
Edward Elgar Publishing Limited
Glensanda House
Montpellier Parade
Cheltenham
Glos GL50 1UA
UK

Edward Elgar Publishing, Inc.
136 West Street
Suite 202
Northampton
Massachusetts 01060
USA

A catalogue record for this book
is available from the British Library

Library of Congress Cataloguing in Publication Data

Down, Simon, 1962–
    Narratives of enterprise : crafting entrepreneurial self-identity in a small firm / Simon Down.
        p. cm.
    Includes bibliographical references.
    1. Entrepreneurship–Psychological aspects. 2. Businesspeople–Psychology. 3. Small business. I. Title.

HB615.D69 2006
658.02'2019–dc22

2005057451

ISBN-13: 978 1 84376 767 1 (cased)
ISBN-10: 1 84376 767 8 (cased)

Printed and bound in Great Britain by MPG Books Ltd, Bodmin, Cornwall

Contents

Cast of characters, names and places

John	Owner-manager, Fenderco
Paul	Owner-manager, Fenderco
Will	Assistant, Fenderco
Mark	Assistant, Fenderco
Fenderco	Paul and John's joint venture company
FendercoEurope	Fenderco's European partner in the joint venture
Jurgen	Managing Director of FendercoEurope
Ausfend	Fenderco's Australian corporate partner in joint venture
Harbourco	Paul and John's employer prior to buyout from EuroPort
EuroPort	Corporate buyers of Harbourco: last employers of Paul and John before starting Fenderco
Steel Applications	One of Paul and John's other related companies
The 'castle house'	Paul's home
The Grinning Cat	Local pub
Maltonbury	Middle-England town where Fenderco is based

Acknowledgements

Like the enterprising activity I describe, this book is both an individual and collective endeavour. Barbara Czarniawska, David Goss, Bob Jones, Eugene Sadler-Smith, Chris Steyaert, Tony Watson and a number of anonymous reviewers have all made major and minor contributions and suggestions. Some of which have been used and some ignored. James Reveley, esteemed colleague and sometime co-author, definitely deserves a pat on the back for pointing out my sometime cavalier attitude to social theory. The resulting text with all its faults is all my doing. I am especially grateful to Paul, John, Will and Mark for their willing engagement in this research. Thanks also to Francine O'Sullivan, Jo Betteridge and all at Edward Elgar for their professionalism in producing this book. For those that have had to endure the writing of this book over all the different houses, countries and years, I save the greatest thanks.

1. Introduction

Jesù writing is hard work all my fingers ake already.
Umberto Eco *Baudolino* (2002: 2)

Anything from the sound of a word through the color of a leaf to the feel of a piece of skin can [...] serve to dramatize and crystallize a human being's sense of self-identity.
Richard Rorty *Contingency, Irony, and Solidarity* (1989: 37)

Eighteen years old and already a Trainee Pop Impresario. Not a job title you'd find pinned to the spongy gray partitions of your local Job Centre. But this is how Simon saw himself; this was his route to becoming someone. Inspired and voyeuristically revolted in equal measure by Malcolm McClaren's prissy art school colonization of DIY boot boy culture, he was captured by the tin foil opportunity of London, loud music and the confidence thin hope of fame and fortune. For this particular small town boy the counter-culture, big city dream had spun its web of fortune round again: he was mobilised, ready for action.

Vicious, Simonon and Joey Ramone. Bass playing was cool, but it wasn't hard in 1979. Hell, John Entwhistle and Bill Wyman were the competition! Okay, it was difficult to actually play with the thing with it dangling round your ankles, but punk facilitated ATTITUDE if not proficiency. With three riffs safety-pinned to his mind, a bag fit for hitching and a quick 'so long suckers' to those that would never leave, Simon followed the Whittington trail to London.

It was hard, managing two work identities. But Simon enjoyed the attention that the record label received from the music press. As the business grew – it made little money, though the bands always whispered and muttered about being ripped off – Simon joined forces with a friend, Paul (Simon's brother, Ed, helped out too). As time and record releases issued forth, Simon and Paul began to feel comfortable with being (very) minor pop entrepreneurs.

Somewhat against the fashions of the time – or at least that was what they said and thought of their studious anti-fashion – they would dress up in dark business suits, ties and sheepskin overcoats. Cheap and flashy cigars would be smoked, and they otherwise attempted to project an image crossed somewhere between Malcolm Allison (a famously sheepskin coated manager of Crystal Palace and Manchester City football teams in the 1970s) and the Kray twins (photographs were even posed for, copying a portrait of theirs). Simon was projecting an image. It was complex, or so he thought, and aimed at cloaking himself with an entrepreneurial confidence, but in a 'psst ... need a new watch or silk stockings?' sense. The 'hard' spivvy image (and the talk that went with it), was consciously orchestrated as counter fashion (remember, at the time the frills of New Romanticism were in popular vogue), a marketing strategy, and intended to install some faith in themselves and

1

the bands they managed. They needed this 'tough' and supposedly sophisticated exterior to cover their immaturity, inexperience and occasional fear when dealing with some of the actually nefarious gig promoters and the like that abound in the music industry.

Simon had created a sense of who he wanted to be. He had made himself a self-identity.

This self-making process is what *Narratives of Enterprise* is about. The above story is intended to introduce the central concept of the book: the narrative construction of self-identity. The story suggests that a large part of the social meaning of who individuals are is created by the juxtaposition of the individual and society; through the interaction of the individual and others.

My purpose in writing this book is to examine the manner in which people – in particular, enterprising people – express and project their self-identities. As will become apparent the approach adopted in this book sees self-identity as something that people create through narrative expression. Because people talk about themselves in relation to other people, things and institutions, narrative expression of self-identity is an inherently social achievement. Thus this book is also focussed on the social contexts in which narratives about self-identity are spoken.

The first few pages of this chapter present a narrative about how I perceive who I was in the past. Within the story are many contexts in which I am placing myself through my narrative. A stance to the institution of work is adopted; the importance of artistic and entrepreneurial expression and desires about self-fulfilment are expressed; I comment on the importance of the way people look and how this can create perceptions of power and control, and so on. Through my beginning with a story, I have also established some cultural and contextual empathy: I have established an age (a teenager at the time of punk), a cultural sensibility (punk, counter-culture, 1970s football, gangsters and the swinging 1960s), a geographical location and my personal experience with entrepreneurial creativity. As a way of introducing a book the narrative also makes an academic and stylistic statement about the sort of writing that follows, and the sort of writer I perceive myself to be. Thus, this part narrative is awash with individual and contextual narratives of self-identity.

This book is not about my entrepreneurial and self-identity however. The research presented in this book is about Paul and John, who are also entrepreneurs and the research subjects of this book. Though others – their assistants Mark and Will, their business partners and others in their work and life histories – feature in the tale I tell, the analytical focus is resolutely on Paul and John and their entrepreneurial self-identities.

Who are these people then? Simply, they are two entrepreneurs who run a small firm in the port fendering business. Prior to starting their firm, 'Fenderco' – a small joint venture firm with larger and corporate partners based in Europe and Australia – they worked together for Harbourco for a number of years. The company is responsible for designing and selling fendering equipment: large steel and rubber structures that are designed to stop ship hulls and wharf sides from being damaged in berthing and manoeuvring procedures. Fenderco is based in Maltonbury, a small fictitiously named market town in middle-England. It is also where the fieldwork that provides the empirical material for this book was conducted. For now however this is enough about Paul and John. Getting to know the research subjects is just one aspect of this introductory chapter. There are other things that need to be said. First something more about the purpose and scope of the book should be addressed.

PURPOSE AND SCOPE OF *NARRATIVES OF ENTERPRISE*

A book on any topic, academic or otherwise, needs to be interesting. Academic books have a duty to be original too. Any story however banal or clichéd will have its new aspects, if for no other reason that the context and setting in which the story is told will necessarily differ. Being interesting is in my mind more important than originality. What is hopefully both, particularly to those interested in entrepreneurs, about this book is that it offers the mostly theoretical discussions of the narrative construction of self-identity more 'bodied stuff' on which to feed (Geertz 1973: 23).

The 'stuff' of this book (Paul and John) is admittedly somewhat limited in terms of the numbers of research subjects investigated, but the analytical objective pursued in *Narratives of Enterprise* demands empirical investigation based on ethnographic research.[1] Ethnography relies on the researcher/writer experiencing, recording and then representing a part of the world, as if they were a stranger; ethnographic studies often make what is familiar seem strange, interesting and helpful in ways they have not been before. The contribution I make therefore is not at the level of aggregated facts. Rather it is in the form of describing, clarifying and creating a vocabulary for certain processes. As Charles Taylor has written, I am making explicit 'the self-understandings that constitute our social life' (1989: 105). The book can be described therefore as empirically informed theorising. Hopefully because of this sustained engagement with just one social context, and the readers' ability to get to know the subjects well, your interest will also be captured and sustained.

In addition, the book adds to our understanding of two things. First, the social and narrative processes of self-identity construction in general are explored through the detail of a particular case. Second, and more importantly given the paucity of long-term qualitative research into entrepreneurial activity, small businesses and the people who work in and run them, the book adds a great deal to our understanding of entrepreneurs. This is not because there are few studies of entrepreneurial behaviour, far from it. Rather it is because there are few investigations of entrepreneurs from the philosophical, methodological and disciplinary perspectives adopted in this book. As a result the study offers a significant new horizon on our sense of what sort of people entrepreneurs can be, and the different ways we might go about thinking and talking about them. This second contribution is more important because this book is mainly offered to readers interested in matters entrepreneurial, though other readers will also find the often difficult to grasp, and oftentimes poorly written, theory on self-identity made clearer through reading this book.

The need for convincing explanations of entrepreneurial activity via interpretive methodologies has almost become a cliché within some of the academic disciplines that are interested in these topics. More studies using these perspectives do seem to be emerging however, as the limits (Grant and Perren 2002) of more traditional philosophies and methodologies have been reached. As far as I am aware, only Dorinne Kondo's (1990) work exploring the crafting of identity in a small Japanese firm has previously focussed on self-identity and small business activity in a similar way.

This is a different book from Kondo's, and not just because it's set in England. The theoretical tools used to explain what was seen, heard and felt whilst in the field, are skewed more towards understanding the individual construction of self-identity, than the identities in the small firm as a whole (Kondo's chief achievement). I am more interested in *entrepreneurial* self-identity than in identities per se.

This emphasis on the individual is not without its broader significance. What does *Narratives of Enterprise* and its new horizon on entrepreneurial agency have to offer? What do the new perspectives I draw upon offer that psychology and economics cannot?

To answer this we need to think historically. The entrepreneur and enterprise have since the early 1980s undergone a profound and arguably politically inspired economic and social resurrection. Whilst scholars argue about the material economic and organisational impact, few would disagree that the rise of enterprise and entrepreneurial rhetoric has profoundly recast the thinking behind the management of most economic and organisational activity, to say nothing of the broader social impacts. In the past notions of the entrepreneur might have suggested heroism, it was just as likely, at least in Europe, to be used as a term of abuse (Burrows 1991: 1). Where people as such were treated at all in mainstream literatures it was exceptional individuals that were seen as the key to understanding entrepreneurial agency. Static theories of economic and psychological behaviour, where people were rational, possessed traits, had essences and had the same inherent motivations and desires, could more or less cope with these exceptions. But what happens when everyone becomes an entrepreneur?

Many argue that the rise of individualism and enterprise over the last three decades means that people in the Western world have become enterprising selves (Rose 1996; du Gay 2000b). This type of talk is often overdone, and there are always arguments between those that see the future in the present and those that see the past: on the topic of enterprise some have suggested that the past was never as unenterprising as it is often made out to be (Curran 1986). The trends today are clear though. Western society is more individualised and privatised; individuals choose or must accept more risk and responsibility in their lives. Even as consumers we are targeted individually. Work has become more transient and enterprising in orientation. We are expected to be more flexible, self-reliant and entrepreneurial at work. Our organisations are changing and becoming less interested in looking after us; we have the 'freedom of insecurity' (Beck 2000: 53). Similar changes are occurring in political and social spheres, and there are many arguments about not just the extent and significance of these changes, but also whether they are good or bad (Sennett 1998).

Some argue (Giddens 1991; Rose 1996; Beck 2000) that the very way we think of being a person is also in the process of transition. As a result of these and other changes in the modern world we are able to, or must, create for ourselves a sense of self. We create our own narrative of who we are; we engage in identity work. We are entrepreneurs of the self.

The broad thrust of this argument is that our times have seen the erosion of many institutions that in the past provided the raw material for the cosseting and buttressing narratives by which people constructed their sense of who they were. If this sense of self is changing such that enterprise is the condition of all, then clearly theories that treat entrepreneurial agents as exceptional are less persuasive or useful (Chapter 2 explains the failings of mainstream economic and psychological explanations of the self in more detail). In societies where all are individuals, all are entrepreneurs, we need theories that can explain how people create themselves in society as unique individuals. This book explains how this is achieved in the case of two small business entrepreneurs: how Paul and John create their narrative self-identity. It treats them not as nascent Schumpetarian superheroes but as everyday exponents of our increasingly enterprising and individually orientated society.

I did not set out with this objective in mind, it emerged from doing the research itself. The original research was focused on how entrepreneurs learn (Down 1999a). As the research (conducted intermittently for two and a half years between 1996 and 1998) progressed the empirical materials I had collected through observation and interviews seemed to say much more interesting things about how Paul and John constructed and maintained a coherent and consistent sense of who they were than they did about learning. Though as Chapter 4 will show self-identity and learning are not unrelated (Down and Reveley 2004).

As the research materials were read, prodded and played with (that means 'analysed' to the professional researchers among you) a sense of order seemed to establish itself around the concept of the narrative construction of self-identity. What made sense to me was the way Paul and John talked about their lives in stories and narratives. The chapter themes – *Relationships*, *Generations*, *Space* and *Clichés* – emerged from this analysis, via a process of either empirical (in that notions of 'relationships' and 'generations' seemed important to the way they talked about themselves) or conceptual ordering (in that the themes seemed to illuminate what they were saying about themselves). Other narratives, and other empirical and conceptual themes did not survive this process, and those offered in Chapters 3–6 do not claim to provide a complete story.

This ordering of my data seemed to throw up the most interesting questions, questions that had not been asked before; questions that might create more persuasive ways of looking at how individuals become (and how society makes) entrepreneurs; and what it means to the individual to sustain that entrepreneurial self.

Two forms of narrative emerged as relevant and useful characterisations of what was seen and heard at Fenderco. There were those stories that Paul and John told about themselves: the events and experiences of their lives. This is what Margaret Somers calls ontological or self-narrative (1994). There were also public narratives used in their talk. These refer to 'those narratives attached to cultural and institutional formations larger than the single individual, [and] to intersubjective networks or institutions' (ibid.: 619). These narratives are not the whole story though. As Somers argues,

> Because neither social action nor institution-building is solely produced through ontological and public narratives, our concepts and explanation must include the factors we call social forces [...]. The challenge [...] is to devise a vocabulary that we can use to reconstruct and plot over time and space the ontological narratives and relationships of historical actors, the public and cultural narratives that inform their lives, and the crucial intersection of these narratives with the other relevant social forces. [ibid.: 620]

From this perspective self-identity is not a categorical essence, tightly held within individuals separate from society. It is a mutable achievement in time, space and through relations with others. Somers along with others (Giddens 1991; Jenkins 1996) have all attempted in various ways to explain the self within a dynamic processual account of society. Self and society are not separate entities in these schemes but different aspects of a social whole.

This book responds in part to Somers' challenge and seeks to produce a clear and useful vocabulary describing the processes inherent in creating entrepreneurial self-identity. This is the overall purpose and value of the work presented here. It is to understand how the entrepreneurial self-identities of Paul and John work in practice. To make explicit some of the self-identity construction and maintenance processes which take place in Fenderco.

In so doing this study and associated work (Down 2002; Down and Reveley 2004; Reveley, Down and Taylor 2004) contributes to our understanding of certain phenomena categorised as knowledge. The book fills certain gaps, and in part responds to certain specific omissions and deficiencies of previous research, particularly in regards to the lack of interpretive empirical research into entrepreneurs and small businesses, as I mentioned earlier. Discussion of the position of this research in regards extant knowledge can wait for the following chapters (especially Chapter 2). What might be useful now, having identified the broad purpose of this book is to identify which audiences or academic disciplines might be interested.

That this identification is necessary is testament to the increasing specialisation of professional practice. There are academic disciplines that would totally reject the assumptions – or more likely, not find in it much value – about individual human beings this book makes. In the next chapter I acknowledge that the genetic and psychophysiological basis for knowing who we are, are fundamentally important, but a different matter from how self-identity is socially mediated and understood. It may come as something of a surprise to some, but recent advances in the scientific understanding of the mind have lent support to those social scientists (many of whom populate this book) who argue that the self is a narrative construction, an abstract 'illusion' created through the evolutionary emergence of consciousness (Dennett 1993).

It is true that some these of these advances also challenge many of the shibboleths of social science and philosophy (see Gray 2003 for instance for a speculative and challenging polemic against universal notions of morality and ethics, based on the new realities of an illusionary and elastic narrative self), but there is some agreement on the basic concepts of self-construction (contrast Giddens's (1991), and Dennett's (1993) notions of self-identity for instance). This book does not attempt to marry social and natural science, though. My task is more specialised and modest.

It is specialised in the sense of how academic knowledge is organised both paradigmatically, and into specific disciplines. Partly through personal temperament and in part through a desire to appeal to a broad audience, I take an eclectic rather than a dogmatic view of incommensurability – the supposed incompatibility of theories. Theoretical purity in the social sciences is often an immature indulgence that creates much misunderstanding, to say nothing of unnecessary and circular debate. Nevertheless this work is situated within, intended for, and articulated with its assumptions in mind, a largely social science audience. More exactly this book operates within the organisational studies and the entrepreneurial and small business fields. And a glance at the references (something that you, if you are an academic, would have already done no doubt) will show where I have situated myself within the disciplines and sub-disciplines that study entrepreneurs, work and organisations.

But in many ways all this really means is that I am trading in fashions (as when I managed bands) and telling of society in a particular way (Becker 1986b). To produce intelligible, situated and legitimate knowledge the author and the reader need at least to understand which paradigm is being operated within. We both need to understand and agree on a few 'very basic, taken-for-granted understandings that form a frame for the conduct of "normal science"' (Giddens 1976: 136). Hopefully, from what has been written so far (I feel as though I have just handed out my intellectual 'business card') this is now clear.

SOME BASIC AND PROVISIONAL DEFINITIONS

There is much, no doubt, which remains unclear. In addition to simply stating what the topic and contribution might be, and to which audiences the book is aimed, the manner in which certain basic ideas, concepts and words are defined should perhaps be provisionally addressed. In this way further boundaries framing this book and the claim to knowledge it makes can of necessity be put in place.

First a general point should be made. The ideas and explanations contained in this book do not offer an abstract theory or technical vocabulary for explaining its topic. The analysis and description in this study draws on the '"mutual knowledge" [that] represent[s] the interpretative schemes which both sociologists and laymen use, and must use, to "make sense" of social activity [and] generate "recognisable" characterisations of it' (Giddens 1976: 161). Neither abstract scientism nor arcane and baroque theoretical deconstruction of everyday terms, only to use them anyway, feature in this work.

There is though a need to engage with definitional debates and avoid the over-simplification that lay terms are often dammed for in academic writing. There are three aspects of this book that need to be at least provisionally defined. These are: what I mean by naming Paul and John 'entrepreneurs', what is meant by 'narrative' and what is meant by 'self-identity'.

The last of these will be dealt with first and simply by saying that self-identity is addressed in detail in Chapter 2. For now the limited and perfunctory understanding that it is something that individuals create through narrative expression via their engagement with society that was sketched earlier will suffice.

What does need some limited clarification is my characterisation of Paul and John as entrepreneurs. The most important aspect of this particular definitional quagmire (see Dibben 2000: 269, for a short and wise discussion of the 'facile debate' over these definitional issues) is that it should be immediately sidestepped. Thankfully the distinction between the terms small business, owner-managers, managers, entrepreneurs and so forth is not a particularly important one in this book beyond their having the status of 'what-everybody-knows' (Silverman 1970: 6). This is not to say that the book is not interested in entrepreneurs and small firms, nor does it ignore previous studies into how people construct an entrepreneurial self (for example Cohen and Musson 2000; Kets de Vries 1977), but it is not the project of this book to refute the theories of other paradigms and disciplines.

In order to address the problem of understanding the narrative processes of self-identity it is not necessary to have a firm and static definition of social roles or categories. I am not interested in what Paul and John *really* are because I argue that what they *really* are is something that they flexibly construct from a combination of the available narratives. That they do claim to be entrepreneurs and define aspects of their self-identity in this way is what is relevant in this book. It is how they narratively go about using talk about being an entrepreneur that interests this investigation.

Finally the term narrative is used to refer to that which is spoken and forms a story, or part thereof. An alternative term 'discursive practice' (Collinson 1992) is on my reading at least, broader and more inclusive[2] in its approach to human utterance. Empirically the term narrative also implies a focus upon the linked and holistic aspects of human speech and action, rather than the much more detailed and minute examination of human speech typified by conversation analysis or semiotics. Thus in this book what Paul and John say and do is part of their story, their self-narrative.

These short outlines are clearly inadequate. The emphasis on narrative, self-identity and of *what* Paul and John are identifying with when they call themselves entrepreneurs are important and raise variously important theoretical issues. Some of these debates are engaged more fully at various points of the book. To say more now would mean a far more elaborate explanation of the approach to self-identity adopted in this book than would be appropriate.

CONCLUSION, STYLE AND PLAN OF BOOK

This chapter has been purposively brief. I have introduced the broad purpose, the main characters of the story and pointed out which audiences might find this work interesting and useful. Some boundaries around my topic have been created through provisionally characterising basic terms and concepts. It is brief also because the impact and substance of this book is very definitely and correctly held within its depths. Ethnographic research does not tend to discover earth-shattering facts. Rather insights emerge through the recounting and mediation of the 'original' experience. The reader cannot easily just know what the point is from reading the introduction and conclusion (though I hope they are nevertheless a reasonable guide) but must engage with the story as it unfolds.

But unfold it does. And before explaining how the book proceeds I should like to say something about the style in which it is written and the spirit offered. The social science concepts of self-identity are not especially accessible as far as much of the literature is concerned. If I have not done justice to the theoretical subtleties of the writers I support, or harm to the theorists rejected, then it is a mostly inadvertent consequence of a desire to maintain readability. I have written elsewhere (Down 2001a) that social science normally struggles to stay in the best-seller lists when it comes to writing popular non-fiction books. This is a shame and it doesn't have to be so. I have tried hard, to the best of my ability, to write about social science theory clearly and simply and to keep Paul and John's inherently interesting story in the forefront. An educated lay reader interested in entrepreneurs and the nature of self-identity should not feel excluded. If this stylistic orientation alienates some academic colleagues then they in my view should examine the purpose that specialist, technical and theory-jargon serves in their field: books are for reading not impressing.

Finally I should outline how this book is structured. The next chapter explains the notion of self-identity and why and how it is useful in researching entrepreneurs. In addition to Chapter 2 explaining the purpose of the empirically based Chapters 3–6 it also establishes the approach to thinking about self-identity I take in this book, which, as outlined above draws upon the work of Somers (1994), Giddens (1991) and others (Jenkins 1996; Sennett 1981; Taylor 1989).

Chapters 3–6 address Paul and John's narratives. The sequence of these chapters loosely follows a narrative chronology based on the formation and consolidation of Paul and John's entrepreneurial venture. These chapters tell a story, characters are developed, settings described. This is not a novel though and I do not shy away from interpretation and analysis; this is an academic work, albeit one that favours readability over theoretical muscularity.

Chapter 3 focuses on the formation and nature of the social relationships in the new firm and the changes in those relationships as the firm becomes established. It looks at the relational dimension: the manner in which they discuss and act towards others and each other and the effect this has on how they create and maintain an entrepreneurial self-identity.

In Chapter 4 – which deals with how events in their past employment histories led them to form Fenderco – the manner in which Paul and John talk about being part of a generation of engineer managers provides an example of the temporal dimension of self-identity narratives (see also Down and Reveley 2004).

Chapter 5 addresses the spatial dimension of how Paul and John construct and maintain their self-identities. It reflects on *where* the narratives as a whole take place and the meaning these narratives of social space have (again, as with Chapter 4 focusing mostly on the present and on events in the immediate past).

In Chapter 6 the empirical analysis turns towards a particular form of language. The way in which Paul and John use public narratives based on entrepreneurial clichés is examined. This chapter lays somewhat askance to the narrative chronological ordering, but in addressing the broader issue of the use of language in creating an entrepreneurial identity it fittingly brackets all of Paul and John's work lives, reflecting even on the distant past and the possible futures.

The final chapter synthesises the themes that emerge throughout the book and brings together some central arguments. It answers the question: what have we learned about entrepreneurs through the notion of narrative self-identity? In so doing I inevitably seek also to broaden the analysis beyond the parochial concerns of empirical research. I briefly explore the relevance of this study to considerations of enterprise in society more generally.

It turns out that what we learn about the entrepreneurs in this story, Paul and John, is that entrepreneurship is a fairly mundane affair. The manner in which individuals – well these individuals at least – create themselves as entrepreneurs is not that mysterious but to a large part based on the strategic mobilisation of narrative resources: something we all do in creating a self-identity. Paul and John use these resources to facilitate entrepreneurial action and provide coherence to their sense of self in a situation (running an entrepreneurial business) which is often fraught with uncertainty.

We learn that their strategy has certain consequences to them as individuals and to the people around them. To maintain this particular entrepreneurial sense of self they end up having to control more than just their business. Relationships to each other and employees, interpretations of past events, the locations they inhabit and the language they use are all controlled, co-opted and marshalled to achieve the coherence they need for their entrepreneurial self-identity.

We also learn that creating an entrepreneurial sense of self and using the narrative resources that help shape that self is something that is easily changed: when circumstances and contexts change self-narratives change too.

Overall this study suggests that we should talk of entrepreneurialism and enterprise in quieter voices. In our rush to heap praise on the impossibly heroic entrepreneurial protagonists that seek out the holy grail of enterprise generated prosperity, or alternatively condemn the pursuit and proliferation of "enterprise" as some monstrous destroyer of civic cohesion, we have lost sight of the durable everyday nature of this activity. It turns out that rather than being superhuman Paul and John are just ordinary folk: this book shows how enterprising activity and the narratives that support it create ordinary, believable, everyday entrepreneurial selves.

NOTES

1. A 'Methodological Appendix' explores the details of the research at the end of the book.
2. Some might say the term is overly inclusive in that it is associated with the notoriously all-encompassing term discourse. See Reed (1998) for a critique of the use of the term discourse in organisational analysis. Reed implies that language and power become omnipotent and over-bearing aspects of human organisation when viewed through the totalising concept of discourse. Discursive practice is used on occasion in this book but only when referring to the broader aspects of human utterance it implies, in contrast to the term narrative.

2.   Self-identities of entrepreneurial practice

In life, a man commits himself, draws his own portrait, and there is nothing but that portrait.
Jean Paul Sartre *Existentialism and Humanism* (1973: 42)

INTRODUCTION

Both esoteric and ubiquitous the notion self-identity[1] is fashionably vague and famously imprecise. Sometimes though, as Anselm Strauss pointed out, such ambiguous terms are needed to 'better look around the corners of [...] problem[s]' (1959: 9). For scholars whose interests lay askance to mainstream sociology the concept is perhaps somewhat daunting. It is nevertheless currently implicated in a panoply of debates in many disciplines, and it would be easy in attempting an explanation to lose sight of the aim of this book: to use self-identity and the associated disciplinary, ontological and epistemological stances it implies to contribute to an emerging vocabulary describing the entrepreneur. An explanation is necessary nonetheless, but the emphasis here is on the social practice involved in producing entrepreneurial self-identity narratives: a particular and descriptive enterprise. To understand that practice something of these stances will have to be explained.

This chapter will make an argument about the best way – that is, best for creating patterns of meaning out of this research – to think about self-identity. There is nothing startlingly innovative in the theoretical approach. I draw on and synthesise much that is current in sociology, social-psychology and organisation studies. What is novel is the application to an entrepreneurial context. In making a new synthesis however, there is sense in which the concept of self-identity is also renewed and changed; re-theorised.

I am keen to emphasise the similarity and areas of consensus between self-identity theorists. This is likely to lead to criticisms of conservatism and simplism from some. There are two reasons in running this risk, one practical the second more theoretical. First, in attempting to speak to entrepreneurial *and* organisational and more general audiences there is a practical need to treat lightly the divisive and occasionally obsessive analytical disputes that characterise healthy intra-disciplinary debate. Second, in preparing this book I was particularly struck by the similarities between diverse disciplines in accepting a narrative constructionist view of self-identity (for example the aforementioned confluence between Dennett 1993, and sociological accounts of narrative self-identity, Giddens 1991; Somers 1994). Whilst much divides views on self-identity the commonalties are substantial.

First however, why is there a need to have a new way of talking about the entrepreneur? Aside from the generalisations already discussed in the previous chapter this analysis turns on the methodological and theoretical deficiencies and missed opportunities of one discipline, and a need for empirical elaboration and clarification in another. An argument is made that enterprise studies needs to adopt different methodological and theoretical approaches to entrepreneurial agency. Organisation studies on the other hand, whilst theoretically and methodologically empathetic, would also benefit from a sustained and substantial empirical study of entrepreneurial selves. The section does not however engage in lengthy critique and refutation, others from which I draw have already made these arguments, I merely outline how this book addresses these deficiencies and opportunities.

An explanation of the concept of self-identity as it is used in this book is then made. First a broad and inclusive approach to understanding self-identity is articulated before addressing wider and related concepts such as how individuals are both agents in the world and subject to it. Clearly the view presented here will emphasise the socially mediated nature of human agency, but some specific theoretical positioning is vital if a clear, relatively secure and convincing rendition of self-identity is to be achieved. This rendition is finally addressed in the last section which summarises the particular terminological and theoretical environment in which self-identity is applied.

Overall in this chapter I discuss many aspects of self-identity that are relevant, and also construct arguments that dispense with others. It provides an explanatory space in which to discuss the research. Though an understanding of ontological and epistemological orientations and a definite sense of what is meant when I write about self-identity will become apparent in this chapter, the approach to entrepreneurial self-identity expounded in this book will be very much embedded in the following chapters. The general approach to self-identity explained in this chapter is that it is explicable through the actual experiences and language of people. Hence this chapter does not meet and resolve the challenges it sets; the rest of the book's engagement with Paul and John's lives does that.

DEFICIENCIES AND OPPORTUNITIES

Scholars wedded to normative economic and psychological perspectives have dominated the study of entrepreneurial agency. This hegemony has had at least two effects. Methodologically, the entrepreneur has been treated as a homogenous archetype: a figure that needs to be boxed in, categorised, counted and objectified to be meaningful and useful. With the exception of the superficial case study approach, sustained expressions of actual entrepreneurial experience are rare. The variety of people, diversity in the forms of enterprise, and social and economic change always seem to defy the definitional boundaries that are essential for this form of knowledge. Theoretically the emphasis has been on identifying traits or attributes that the archetypical entrepreneur exhibits and possesses. As a result, whilst research traditions in this vein have usefully provided the statistically amenable identifiers and tools of a whole range of entrepreneurial attributes, the vocabulary of meaning produced has crucial *explanatory* limits. Social scientific understandings of individual behaviour seem to move on but entrepreneurial persons under extant explanatory schemes have to rely on flawed and eclipsed concepts.

Methodologically the arguments for a more processual, interpretative and qualitative understanding of entrepreneurial behaviour are well rehearsed and need not be repeated here (Curran and Burrows 1987: 8; Burrows and Curran 1989: 28, 31; Ogbor 2000). Even those drawing from more deductive positivist logics have encouraged a greater diversity of methods (Low and MacMillan 1998; Bygrave 1989). Calls continue to be made for enterprise scholars 'to step outside the hegemony of their "normal" paradigm and to consider alternative paradigmatic positions' (Grant and Perren 2002: 202). These calls to look beyond normal science ontology and epistemology reflect broader and pervasive shifts in the social sciences, and enterprise studies have arguably been somewhat slow to respond, when compared even to other business-related subjects such as human resource management, for instance.[2]

Whether one views the development of a more interpretative representation of entrepreneurial behaviour as complementary, antagonistic or heterodox, it is difficult to deny its growing presence.

The calls have not gone unheeded though, and in recent years there have been diverse and growing numbers of ethnographic or substantial and sustained interpretative studies into the smaller organisation and the people that manage and work in them (Hobbs 1988; Kondo 1990; Ram 1994; Holliday 1995). They remain a rarity and importantly at the margins of the mainstream disciplines. Notwithstanding the continuing prejudice against philosophical diversity in research, and aside from its inherently time consuming nature, one further reason for this rarity is the particular difficulty associated with getting to do the research. Difficulty in gaining access can be shown in the way that many of these studies, and this one, rely on extant friendships and/or family contacts, and a generally opportunistic and entrepreneurial approach (including covert research, Moule 1998).

The lack of quality research is not surprising when there is so much so-called qualitative research that remains attached to inappropriate 'unit counting' approaches (Curran and Burrows 1987: 8; see Ackroyd 1996, for a broader discussion of this unfortunate misappropriation); which even undermines otherwise useful and sophisticated research (see my review of Dibben 2000 for instance, Down 2001c). It is fair to say therefore in summary that despite the increase in theoretical and methodological imagination, understandings of processes in entrepreneurial and smaller organisations remain underdeveloped. Thus in addition to the specific and innovative understanding of entrepreneurial self-identity that this book offers, it also responds more generally to this need.

It is theoretically however that the need is greater. Clearly from what has been written so far self-identity is in limited respects an analogue of the term personality, albeit from a very different intellectual tradition and with very different analytical implications. Personality is the term that cognitive-psychology attributes to specific and relatively consistent qualities and traits of individuals. Debates about the best way to conceptualise the self and individual behaviour currently abound within social-psychology, and the personality theories of old seem overly reliant on an 'individualistic-objectivist' cognitive view (the phrase is Yvette Lewis's 2003: 228), and are unable to counter contemporary critiques. There seems to be little room in the notion personality to allow for the social construction of the self through the use of language however that process is theorised.

I am not qualified to criticise cognitive-psychology. The particularly reductive manner in which personality theory has and continues to be applied to entrepreneurial behaviour is a different manner, and many enterprise scholars have pointed out the fundamentally flawed nature of the personality trait approach (Gartner 1989; Goss 1991: 49–50; Reynolds 1991: 14; Gray 1998: 151; Mitchell et al. 2002). Indeed, when one reads contemporary work on entrepreneurial personality (see Littunen 2000 for example) one is struck by the manner in which social science appears trapped in time, like some unfortunate insect preserved in amber. There seems to have been little attempt by such scholars to go beyond McClelland (1961) and Rotter et al. (1972).

Even when enterprise scholars do acknowledge the limits of the trait approach, as in the current enthusiasm for 'entrepreneurial cognition' (Mitchell et al. 2002), the approach seems unable and unwilling to deal seriously with society and continues to treat the individual as a relatively unchanging category. Entrepreneurial cognition approaches seem oblivious to the philosophical doubts that other social scientists currently grapple with.

If entrepreneurial cognition is in its infancy however, then notions of narrative identity applied to the entrepreneur are just starting to cause morning sickness, and it would be indulgent to attempt to close off different horizons. The character of the entrepreneur and the processes of entrepreneurship (as a broad social and economic phenomenon), as a way of describing our enterprising spirit, is again important in the world, and now is not the time to legislate against the different languages and vocabularies being used to describe what is happening.

Simplistic use of personality traits theories however is certainly not appropriate. Perhaps their continued use is not surprising given the largely economic concerns of many enterprise studies journals and the consequently subordinate place of individual behaviour in the 'overall' scheme of study. It is true that there have been attempts to respond to the call (Reynolds 1991: 66) to conceptualise individual entrepreneurial behaviour from a more social constructionist perspective (for example Chell et al. 1991), but these have tended to emphasise social context in isolation and have not used developments in identity or narrative/discursive conceptualisations of individuals. This book aims to redress these theoretical deficiencies and joins with others at the margins to try to help resurrect the insect à la Jurassic Park (Cohen and Musson 2000; Fletcher 2003; Hjorth and Steyaert 2004; Warren 2004).

My affinity and empathy with organisational theoretical approaches (and social science more generally) has already been acknowledge and the second purpose of this section is to suggest how this book complements and adds to a range of work by organisationally oriented scholars – the others mentioned above. The purpose is not to explore the debates themselves, which are significant and relevant to the study of entrepreneurs and small organisations (some of which will be engaged at various more appropriate points in the discussion). My objective here is simply to argue that there is a need for specific and substantial empirical studies for organisational scholars interested in issues relating to entrepreneurial selves and behaviour.

Looked at from the distance required for the current purpose there are two subject areas where this book makes a significant contribution. First I bring more of that rare bodied stuff into enterprise culture/discourse debates. Interest in enterprise culture/discourse reflects shifts in economic structures and a consequent reshaping of organisational relationships. These changes in economic history have also been conterminous with academic fashions that favour difference and the particular over universality. As a result the general climate of sociological and organisational research has become increasingly pluralistic and inclusive of non-standard organisational subjects, including the smaller organisation. This book provides interpretative empirical material about the manner in which people go about entering the enterprise culture and how they articulate their engagement with it. There are two strands to this literature.

There are those scholars whose interests lay at the political and social implications of the rise of the enterprise culture (Curran and Stanworth 1984; Keat and Abercrombie 1990; Curran 1990; Goss 1991; Burrows 1991; Curran and Blackburn 1991, 1994; Gray 1998), and those organisational scholars interested in the rise and use of the discourse (Fournier and Grey 1999; du Gay 2000a; Cohen and Musson 2000: 31; Ogbor 2000). In these debates the level of analysis is focused on shifts in the overall characteristics of organisational and social life: specifically whether or not organisations and society are more or less enterprising as a result of structural and discursive changes *in toto*. My book cannot comment directly but all debates need descriptive content to work from and the research presented here provides a theoretically empathetic vocabulary for understanding some important individual processual elements.

Second, and very briefly as we need to get started, in addition to issues of entrepreneurial interest, the empirical focus will also be of interest more broadly to those organisational scholars beginning to research the relationships between narrative, discourse and identity in the context of work and organisations (Kondo 1990; Collinson 1992; Watson 1994; Alvesson 1994; Rose 1996; Parker 2000; Kärreman and Alvesson 2001; Alvesson and Willmott 2002). I stress the empirical contribution not to undermine the explanatory power of this book but to emphasise the parochialism of my theoretical interests.

There are good reasons then to suppose that this study and the arguments it makes about how entrepreneurial agency might be better conceptualised via a narrative concept of self-identity, will be useful to enterprise and organisation scholars alike. Our current understanding of self-identity in this book is not yet sufficient for the task. It is to this we now turn.

SELF-IDENTITY: DEFINITIONS, ANTECEDENTS AND VARIOUS OTHER GOSPELS

A good place to start an explanation of self-identity is to attempt a provisional definition. The need for definition is not merely to assuage indistinction or to sloth after convention. It is part of how we create knowledge. Social science itself is a continual process of defining and naming with the occasional and partial pauses of breath when topics are declared defined for reason of intellectual arrogance, exhaustion or boredom. Self-identity must be created or made into an object to become something, to be explicable. But the object does not have an 'essence' in itself; it 'is dependent on how it is defined by the namer' (Strauss 1959: 20). As Giddens has noted

> to know the meaning of words is to use them [...]. We come to know reality not

from perceiving it as it is, but as a result of the differences formed in daily practice. To come to know the meaning of the word 'table' is to get to know what a table is used for, which implies also knowing how the use of a table differs from other functional objects. [1991: 43]

Thus individuals (you and me both) don't really need or use the various definitional parameters and components of identity that social science creates to be able to live and make sense of our lives. For most of us it is an easy and fluid part of our daily lives. Our compounded nouns and phrases that form sociological concepts are blunt instruments. Just as with Flaubert's take on human speech, sociological concepts are mostly 'like a cracked kettle on which we strum out tunes to make a bear dance, when we would move the stars to pity' (1975: 203).

To say anything sensibly however knowing as exactly as one can what is being discussed is vital. We need to move beyond the given definition that self-identity is the sense of knowing that we are someone, that we can identify ourselves as that someone, and that others also identify that self-same someone. Giddens's definition is often used and a good place to start

> Self-identity is not a distinctive trait, or even a collection of traits, possessed by the individual. It is *the self as reflexively understood by the person in terms of her or his biography*. [...]. A person's identity is not to be found in behaviour, nor – important though this is – in the reactions of others, but in the capacity *to keep a particular narrative going*. [1991: 53–4, original emphasis]

Giddens thus stresses the ability to create a story (or many different but related stories) of one's self over and above what people *do* and how they *interact* with others (though they need to interact to have self-identity is indubitably the case).

Somers suggests that this narrative constitution of identity has four interrelated dimensions; two of which concern us here.[3] 'Ontological narratives [...] are the stories that social actors use to make sense of – indeed, to act in – their lives' (Somers 1994: 618). These narratives make up the stuff of our 'selfy selves' (Dennett 1993: 416). Ontological narratives must come from somewhere; they cannot be self-generating. They rely on interpersonal and social interaction over time and hence are sustained and transformed by another dimension of narrative: 'Public narratives are those narratives attached to cultural and institutional formations larger than the single individual, to intersubjective networks or institutions, however local or grand, micro- or macro-stories about American social mobility, the "freeborn Englishman," the working-class hero' (Somers 1994: 619). We might add the 'entrepreneur'.

According to Somers our production of narratives transforms the random events and experiences of individuals' temporal and spatial relationships with others into episodes. We already know that self-identity is the capacity to keep a particular narrative going: being able to selectively appropriate the multifarious events and experiences of life and 'emplot' (the ability to create a plausible and intelligible plot or story line) them according to particular themes. We must in some way discriminate between 'the infinite variety of events, experiences, characters, institutional promises, and social factors that impinge on our lives' (Somers 1994: 617). These emploted themes provide consistency in our narratives and are themselves dependent on having 'an evaluative framework' which is shaped by 'a set of fundamental principles and values' (ibid.). The reason for adding this moral imperative to our conception of self-identity can best be stated by quoting Taylor

> because we cannot but orient ourselves to the good, and thus determine our place relative to it and hence determine the direction of our lives, we must inescapably understand our lives in narrative form, as a 'quest'. [...]. I see these conditions as connected facets of the same reality, inescapable structural requirements of human agency. [1989: 51–2][4]

Self-identity has been defined and given some analytical dimensions. We can summarise the above by saying that there are three distinct and underlying conditions of self-identity: identity as stories being made (narratives), identity as relations with others in time and space and identity as moral choice. This chapter needs to do far more than this. The above definition and tentative elaboration evaporates a large and broad debate. What follows below is a further elaboration of the concept of self-identity, and how it has been variously sub-divided, categorised or characterised. In the following section the theoretical implications (particularly in regards agency, structure, discourse and subjectivity) of looking at the self in this way are further explored.

*

Different academic disciplines, historical eras and national traditions have used a variety of terms to describe what I broadly understand to mean by self-identity. The 'self' for instance, has been used for centuries. It seems to imply a more abstract and philosophical notion when compared to the use of the more mundane and utilitarian 'identity'. The 'self' seems far more related to the general state of individual being. In Casey's work for instance the self is an abstract and general notion: as in the nature of 'all selves' in society as a result of industrialism (1995: 51). Other terms such as the 'person', 'selfhood', 'personhood', and 'self-understanding' (Brubaker and Cooper 2000) confuse the issue further.

What *is* clear is the disciplinary, ontological and epistemological gulf between those who use 'personality' and 'identity'. Critics of the term personality agree (Davies and Harré 1991; Potter and Wetherell 1987) that its use implies a fixed unified entity that people *have*. There is no need to extend this debate further than I have already done so earlier discussing entrepreneurial personality. Except to note that Kärreman and Alvesson's dismissal of 'depth-psychological' identity issues in favour of a narrower focus on 'work/occupational/organisation based personal and group identities', which can 'arguably' be understood more through a socially constructed view of human subjectivity (2001: 63) is also adopted here.

It should be noted however that the demarcation of the social from the 'inner' depth-psychological and physiological is likely to be an analytical convenience. Daniel Dennett's theory of consciousness in particular suggests that the reality of selves is that they are narrative abstractions. Consciousness and having a self is a consequence of having a brain that has developed via evolution the 'good trick' of language and culture. As Dennett notes, 'our tales are spun, but for the most part we don't spin them; they spin us' (1993: 418). In other words our self-identities are created through our distinctive use of language. Dennett is intent on laying to rest the Cartesian separation of the mind from the body, and explains how consciousness is constituted via our interaction with culture, society, evolution and our biology. Having a self-identity is one strategy we employ: 'Each normal individual of this species makes a *self*. Out of its brain it spins a web of words and deeds. [...] This web protects it' (ibid.: 416).

If what Dennett is suggesting seems surprisingly similar to the sociological orthodoxy of narrative identity (Giddens 1991; Somers 1994), it is perhaps even more surprising that sociology and this brand of philosophy seem mutually ignorant of each other's work.[5] The sociological literature has come to similar conclusions about the nature of self-identity, but may eventually need to avoid separating the social from the 'depth-psychological' and physiological. Thus, inherent within much sociological debate is the assumption that we create self-identities on top of psycho-physiological drives to attain a sense of ontological security and thus avoid existential anxiety. These features are seen as the foundation, or to borrow a phrase used above, the 'depth-psychological' (Kärreman and Alvesson 2001: 63), on which we construct our self-identities. Giddens (1991) argues that this is what underlies identity construction. There is therefore an implicit concession to some sort of physiological/psychological/social hierarchy to the production of self-identity, and importantly a 'separation' between the mechanical search for security and the reflexive and 'more' socially constructed domain of motive or value. In other words what takes place largely in childhood where the attainment of security and lack of anxiety normally produces a 'natural attitude' (ibid.: 36), happens in a different, less reflexive manner. The implications of Dennett are not that these foundational drives don't exist, but that there is a greater degree of plasticity and fluidity, not a separation, between them and the socially constructed dimensions of self-identity.

However, whilst these caveats should be borne in mind – the implications of Dennett's (and others) work for our understanding of the reality of selves are far reaching and still just at their beginning – the point of Kärreman and Alvesson and the sociological approach is that we are more *interested* in how individuals *socially* construct their self-identity, rather than its psychology, physiology or evolution. These distinctions however (and this has been the point of this slight digression) are made, not inherent to the subject (see also Kondo 1990: 34).

One of the major parameters of self-identity is the sense of 'difference' from and 'similarity' with others that an individual makes reference to in establishing an identity. Difference from and similarity with others is an inherent and fundamental aspect of our self-development, as we discover the difference between 'me' and 'not me' (Giddens 1991; Dennett 1993: 414). This well understood characteristic of identity (Jenkins 1996: 3–4; Kärreman and Alvesson 2001: 61) has tended to produce a separation of identity into individual/personal identity and collective/social identity. This is now thought to be better explained via theories that in various ways seek to synthesise the individual and society under one explanatory framework (aspects of these theories are elaborated in the next section).

Some have suggested however that identity is anyway too vague and flexible a notion (Brubaker and Cooper 2000). Given the ubiquity of its current use (Bendle 2002) the caution is timely. I agree with Kärreman and Alvesson however who note 'there are no compelling reasons "finally" to resolve the ambiguity of identity. Frankly, it is both potentially fruitful and economical to have a concept that is capable of addressing sameness and difference at the same time' (2001: 62): it's good for looking round the corners of problems. As with other inherently ambiguous terms, such as religion, race (and so on) they are useful and indispensable in academic practice. This reflects the need for the social scientists to engage with, not reject, the 'mutual knowledge' that 'represent the interpretative schemes which both sociologists and laymen use, and must use, to "make sense" of social activity [and] generate "recognisable" characterisations of it' (Giddens 1976: 161). Social life *is* ambiguous, contradictory, paradoxical and so on.

Part of that mutual knowledge regarding similarity between people consists of what MacIntyre's has described as 'characters'. He argues that there are well-established characters in society that act as 'social roles which provide a culture with its moral definitions' (1981: 29). He suggests that characters are moral reference points. The confluence here with Somers's notion of public narrative is obvious. Characters such as the bureaucratic manager or indeed the entrepreneur, are public narratives that help provide part of the evaluative criteria needed to make narrative identity. As will become apparent – particularly in Chapter 6 – Paul and John draw on the 'character' of the entrepreneur and its associated moral definitions to construct their sense of self-identity. They are not just performing the role of the entrepreneur. They also have a particular interpretative relationship to the 'character' of that role which they articulate through language, and which produces certain moral justifications about their activities: 'bureaucrats are bad for business. I am more enterprising than that. I must be a good person'. As we shall see later both Paul and John include this type of talk in their narratives.

MacIntyre's use of 'character' helps us explain an important difference between social role and self-identity. Discussing the character of the trade-union official he notes that 'the beliefs that he has in his mind and heart are one thing; the beliefs that his role expresses and presupposes are quite another' (ibid.: 28). From MacIntyre's comments it is clear that role narrowly depicts a sense of self that is 'static, formal and ritualistic' (Davies and Harré 1991: 43). This is not to suggest that roles do not exist or that they do not provide material with which to construct public and other narratives. The term role does however tend to assume a prime status for the narrative equipment of a category over the situated and enacted narrative of individuals. Roles such as mother or entrepreneur are often treated as fixed models rather than being narratively constructed and historically contingent, as MacIntyre's use of 'character' implies.

The historical and temporal contingency absent in the term role raises another important feature of self-identity. We have seen that it encompasses what people are not as well as what they are. This implies that an individual can move towards as well as away from certain self-identities. Self-identity is thus both a static and dynamic aspect of human experience that reflects the life course of individuals.[6] Inherently therefore, there is a transience about understanding our selves and how others see us which is *not* captured by the term role.[7]

This discussion has so far centred on the use of generic terms to describe self-identity: establishing conceptual sameness. A further aspect relates to how others have coined alternative terms to describe self-identity: establishing conceptual difference. A plethora of compound nouns have emerged over the years as social science has attempted to elaborate its understanding of (or more properly, propagate a vocabulary for) identity. If one limits the analysis and ignores the various social, political, gender, class and cultural identities,[8] even with what I am defining as self-identity, a wide range of alternative terms have been used.[9]

We need not go into this here. The next section argues that self-identity and social identity should be viewed as part of the same process of identification.

The chapters that follow show Paul and John creating boundaries between what they feel similar to and what they feel different from. This is a self-identity they are constructing but it is as much a social identity too: they feel part of an entrepreneurial community as well as feeling themselves unique individuals. The public narratives they draw upon to create this identity are social resources. Paul and John use narratives identifying themselves with class, gender, ethnicity, lifestyle, even age social identities. To be sure, I place less emphasis on these but they are important nonetheless. Conceptual narratives also need their limits and boundaries.

We have done the hard work of defining and giving some depth and scope to self-identity as it will be used. This book seeks only to add to an understanding of self-identity at the practical level, by applying and elaborating a vocabulary to describe certain processes. As with Jenkins my 'focus is firmly on the mundane; on how social identity *works*, on the interactional constitution of identity' (1996: 12, emphasis in the original). Some of the relevant ideas, terms, concepts and debates above are engaged later, as are the more entrepreneurially specific literatures. For now a semblance of *what* is being discussed in terms of self-identity should be sufficiently apparent. As I have promised a few times already however, there is a need to discuss further a few theoretical issues before pushing on.

SELF-IDENTITY, AGENCY AND STRUCTURE, DISCOURSE AND SUBJECTIVITY

So far I have emphasised the consensus among those that would accept the notion of narrative self-identity. I think it is right to make this emphasis. I have also given reasons why this book will treat lightly intra-disciplinary analytical disputes. There are however disputes at a higher theoretical level (that is, less related to the empirical and more to the logic of ideas) that require engagement that I have so far discussed only in passing.

Subsumed within the high degree of practical consensus about what self-identity describes are the common fault-lines of debate found in other areas of organisational and sociological analysis. These debates turn on two inter-related and perennial problems. The first is how to conceptualise social agency and structure. The second is how to think about language in relation to society. Part of the reason why social theorists have been so fascinated by self-identity is its very relevance and promise in creating meaningful vocabularies for conversations on these problems. Both have attracted a range of meta-theoretical contributions, which might be crudely rendered as positions on an axis.[10]

At one end you have those that see agency, structure and language as more or less real and separate phenomenon (realists, structuralists). On the other there are those that collapse these distinctions within the discourses that produce them (post-structuralist, post-modernists, radical social-constructionists). There are many points in-between these caricatures that in their pure versions have the appearances of being incommensurable (and often incomprehensible!). Thankfully this is not a work of social or organisational theory and our purpose in looking at these debates at all is to show the fluidity of what we are dealing with when we try to fix meaning to concepts such as self-identity. Crucially it is also to acknowledge that I am trying to fix a position along the axis. To be sure, mine is not a particularly strongly held or well-defended: in trying to explain my position it's often difficult to avoid feeling like the recently spun blindfolded child at a birthday party that must pin the donkey's tail! As I have noted earlier the audience for this book is a mixed one and does not require global positioning satellite technology. An old fashioned atlas will do the job. But positioned we must be if we are to have some way of framing the descriptive analysis which follows and the vocabulary used to express it.

I have written already that recent shifts in social theory regarding structure and agency have meant that the analytic divide between self-identity and social identity has been bridged. Scholars have made serious attempts in recent years to rein-in the conceptual proliferation dividing types of identity to realise the 'entangled' (Jenkins 1996: 19) nature of self and society. Jenkins for instance, attempts to collapse the division between the social and individual identities into one dialectic explanatory framework (ibid.: 17–38). Given that Giddens has provided some of the impetus to this recognition of the unnecessary polarisation between society and the individual (1984; Bourdieu 1977, has done similar, and Berger and Luckmann made an earlier attempt [1965]1991), it is obvious that implicit in his use of the term self-identity (1991) is an understanding that the structure/agency divide is an analytic and practical discursive convenience. Giddens does this by arguing that people in reflexively pursuing and creating their self-identity also produce and reproduce social structures. This is because a 'structure is not a "group", "collectivity" or "organisation": these have structures. Groups, collectivities and so on, can and should be studied as systems of interaction' (1976: 121). Because of the narrative base to this process some have added the term narrative identity to the debate (Somers 1994). In various ways these authors accept the materiality of social forces. What they try to avoid however is the reification of agency and structure into separate essential categories;[11] they emphasise the relational and discursive production and reproduction of systems of interaction.

Post-structural analyses have also been a fundamental part of these attempts to collapse the categorical distinctions between self and society, agency and structure. Michel Foucault and followers have developed a distinctive approach with a particular vocabulary. It has not been adopted here. The area on the axis on which these particular debates lie is very crowded however and the distinctions between Jenkins, Somers and Giddens and the post-structuralist writers such as Kondo and Casey are not greater than their similarities. They happily cite each other's work engaging in stimulating and mostly useful conversations, whilst pointing to their disagreements. The distinctions remain however and a brief discussion is useful.

The different ways in which non-categorical and non-reified renderings of self/agency and society/structure are achieved do have some significant implications. A key issue between these theorists is the role of language; *how* does it produce society, agency and structure? And if it doesn't, what does?

On the one hand there are the critical realist, structuralist, materialist positions (Reed 1997, 2000 are good organisation studies examples of critical realism and see Archer et al. 1998 more broadly). These approaches remain wedded to the idea that there is a reality out there that is independent of the way in which we describe it through language. In terms of the self, realists have been criticised as being unable to avoid a separated and dualistic self and society. The problem then becomes how one bridges the gap between them; what social processes produce selves? How does individual agency produce structure? The individual person also becomes trapped as an objective essence, which we have already seen creates static and socially isolated selves.

On the other hand the post-structuralists and radical social-constructionists emphasise the socially constitutive power and control inherent to discourses or discursive practices themselves. Foucault romantically saw modern society as having taken an unfortunate course into domination and subjugation and away from potential human emancipation. Central to this was the manner in which power and knowledge techniques were reproduced via discourses. Crucially these techniques of categorisation – such as those generated by psychology and medical science – make individuals into subjects. Becoming a subject 'categorizes the individual, mark him by his own individuality, attaches him to his own identity' (1982: 212). Being an individual self was not inherent to nature but historically and discursively specific. Importantly Foucault perceived the manner in which language produced power and that they were not the product of objective social structures; discourse was structure, discourse was power.

The post-structuralist perspective has its own problems. Chief of these is what has happened to the self as practicing embodied agent. Burkitt has asked the question, 'who writes the texts in which the subject appears. [...] What is missing [...] is any notion of *practice* in respect of the formation of discourses and text' (1994: 13, emphasis in the original). The individual does not just conform to language rules and discourses but acts and creates. The self as agent seems to disappear. Many others have made this critique. We need not elaborate and list them.

How then do we deal with this problem? Can we resolve these seemingly incommensurable approaches to language, agency and society? Are structures real? Is there simply language? Much in social science and organisational theory in the last twenty years or so have been attempts to negotiate a way out of this problem. Among the more recent attempts to resolve it in organisation studies is an emerging approach called discursive pragmatism (the term is Alvesson and Kärreman's 2000).

Their thinking is derived from the pragmatism of Richard Rorty who argues that only language can be true or false and that objects have no meaning except through our descriptions. The consequence of this is that because the way we describe things changes over time according to whatever convinces the majority or dominant at the time, we cannot achieve a truthful representation of what is out there in the world. Similarly Rorty's approach 'turn[s] against theory and towards narrative'; it gives up 'the attempt to hold all the sides of our life in a single vision, to describe them with a single vocabulary' (1989: xvi). It does this because truthful knowledge cannot be one thing just a version of it.

Tsoukas has taken this approach into organisation studies (along with Alvesson and Kärreman 2000; and Watson 1997) and shown that there is a way out of this impasse. It is worth quoting him at length

> we should reject the epistemological rivalry between realism and social constructivism [...]. An anti-representionalist account of knowledge, such as provided by pragmatists and interpretivist philosophers, retains the causal independence of the world, while upholding the manifold descriptions the world lends itself to. We are realists simply because reality is where is [sic] has always been, outside our heads. Insofar as we create structures through patterns of sustained interaction [...] we are confronted by real structures [...]. Such structures cause us to form beliefs about them. In turn our descriptions of these structures (more precisely, how we describe them), are matters which depend on the language-based institutionalised meanings a community of actors have historically adopted. [2000: 534]

Language does not represent reality; it expresses a reality. There cannot be one true theory of entrepreneurial self-identity. Tsoukas argues that both the constructionists and the realists make the mistake (one through over-determining objects, the other language) of seeing knowledge as representing reality rather than being a rendition of it. If we are not intent on producing or proposing illusionary fundamental truths about entrepreneurial self-identity, this means we must limit our projects to the production of narratives – if you must, 'theories' – which discuss the processes and contingency-shaped constructions that take place over time and through space. The language I use is one that sees the self as generated through engagement with others. The approach to language I find most useful is where organisational participants have agential discretion in producing narratives among a plurality of mediating discourses that include relationships of power but also include other inter-subjective phenomena and material factors. Language in this approach can also be seen as functioning

> as menus of *discursive resources* which various social actors draw on in different ways at different times to achieve particular purposes – whether these be specific interest-based purposes or broader ones like that of making sense of what is happening in the organisation or what it is to 'be a manager.' [Watson 1995: 816–17, emphasis in the original]

Or, indeed, what it is to 'be an entrepreneur'. This is a wholly more pragmatic and less philosophically puritanical approach to discourse and narrative and agency.

However, when faced with alternative insightful contributions from a range of meta-theoretical and philosophical positions what can one do but use them pragmatically and eclectically? For example, I disagree with the power dominated theoretical basis of Kondo's study but nevertheless I have found it stimulating, incisive and extremely useful for this study, especially in pointing out the practical advantages of a holistic view of the society/self dualism. We are having a conversation about the world. About how we describe those people in society that we call entrepreneurs; about how this type of person creates themselves as entrepreneurs. There isn't just one way of doing this. How useful will my way be? I don't know. The stance adopted in this book follows the spirit of what Mills has written: 'To be mastered by "method" or "theory" is simply to be kept from working, from trying, that is, to find out about something that is going on in the world' ([1959]2000: 121, see also 32–3).

CONCLUSION: THEORY IN PRACTICE

I started this chapter simply by pointing out some reasons why this book might be a good idea and who might find it of interest. In the last two sections I have tried to describe the general confluence of ideas on self-identity and some of the more specific divergences which centre on the irresolvable problems of agency and structure, discourse and subjectivity. I hope the line I have plotted along the axis has been clear and straight, and the place I have set up camp on it amenable. I still feel uncomfortable and unclear about much myself. Part of my argument is intended to suggest that it's all right to feel and think in this way. Social science terms often remain battlegrounds where categorisers and universalists front up against characterisers and particularists (Davis 1971). Why should self-identity or this book be any different? The term 'self-identity' with all its failings *is* the term being used to discuss self-under-standing, subjectivity or the 'selfy self' (Dennett 1993). It's not going to go away: even enterprise scholars have started using it! All conversations about human society are inherently ambiguous and contested and it is as well that we encourage imaginative exploration. Imagination and creativity as much as codification and organisation, are important for achieving human ends; particularly entrepreneurial ones.

In summary therefore I have argued that:

- individual human beings have a sense of self to differentiate themselves from others and other things; this is needed to provide ontological and physical security and protection
- self-identity is a reflexive capacity to construct a biographical narrative, to create a thematic plot out of lived experience
- ontological and public narratives are constructed and drawn upon to create self-identity
- the construction of narrative self-identity is an inherently evaluative process – in that individuals selectively appropriate narratives – and hence linked to moral agency
- self-identity is transient and elastic but coherent and consistent over time and through space
- self-identity is more than the adoption of social roles and attributes of collectivities, and though roles/memberships and other engagement with society add resource content to an individuals' narratives, individual performance and evaluative agency is required to make a narrative self-identity
- self-identity is a relational construct reliant on individual engagement with others and society
  - individual agency and social structure is understood as constitutive of each other
  - but both individuals and social forces are real and not reducible to discourse or text
  - language is an expression not a representation of reality
- narratives and discourses are used as a resource in crafting self-identity

It is within these parameters that this study will operate. As I said earlier my approach to self-identity draws on existing theory. Becker (1986a) has insightfully observed that thankfully most social scientists don't need to start from scratch. Most of the time appropriate theories and concepts have already been developed and can be applied in new social contexts. This research is no different and has happily plundered other theorists' ideas.

This chapter has adopted a systematic and explanatory scheme. It has not rolled-out the various specific concepts that will help explain what Paul and John say and do in relation to the dimensions of narrative identity and other social contexts. This postponement, aside from the lack of clarity that their inclusion here would bring, reflects a desire to be serious about doing justice to the complexities of Fenderco. To discuss these concepts in abstract isolation of their observed contexts would be wrong. As Gergen has suggested 'In the act of theorising, one translates experience into symbol, and the conceptual replica is inevitably a distortion of such experience' (1978: 1357). How much more distorted would the various concepts I use be if they were represented and developed in abstract isolation away from the experience?

It is also important to reassert that the concepts I use and develop in this book are not intended in a categorical or essentialist manner (Somers 1994: 621). I hope that all the concepts used in this book characterise, in that they 'locate people within a processual and sequential movement of relationships and life episodes' (ibid.: 624), more than they categorise. This characterisation is not embodied in the concepts themselves but in their juxtaposition to the observed and conversational realities of Paul and John's lives, located within the narrative dimensions of self-identity. Thus, concepts may seem blunt (like 'cracked kettles' if you will) but underlying them is an appreciation of more subtle interactions between space and time, which Somers and Jenkins argue are central to an understanding of identity (1996: 27). It is the explanatory framework in this chapter in conjunction with the conceptualised interpretations of observed reality in Chapters 3–6 which develops a vocabulary for describing how people go about crafting self-identity in the everyday practice of Fenderco. It is to these chapters, Paul and John's stories, we turn now.

NOTES

1. Though the terms 'self-identity' and 'identity' are used interchangeably hereafter it is only to avoid unnecessary repetition. All identities are inherently social in nature (Jenkins 1996: 4). My use of self-identity or identity does not imply that 'social identity' is of a different order. It merely seeks to emphasise selfness, 'selfhood' (ibid.: 20), or 'self-understanding' (Brubaker and Cooper 2000), and avoid comparison with those who use the term social identity to exclusively denote specific and stereotypical social groupings (based on gender, sexual preference, ethnicity and so on) (see Kärreman and Alvesson 2001: 61).
2. A recent assessment of the state of entrepreneurship studies argued that 'the use of theoretical concepts and analytical tools was limited' (Bessant et al. 2003: 55) and that there was a need to improve the quality of theory-driven research (Low and MacMillan 1998, cited in Bessant et al., 2003).
3. Somers refers to ontological, public, conceptual and metanarratives (1994: 617). The latter

two of these refer first, to the narratives that social scientists use to conceptualise the social landscape, and second, to those narratives which form the base of modern societies ('Progress, Decadence, Industrialisation, Enlightenment etc', ibid.: 619).

4. This is not to say that Giddens ignores morality (1991: 8–9). Far from it. He is perhaps keener to emphasise the space that has emerged between individual action (and the sense of self) and 'moral issues' as a result of the institutional rationality of modernity (ibid.). Whereas Taylor's position though similar in respects the narrative, quest-like nature of selfhood, prefers to see self-identity as explicitly and 'inextricably intertwined' with the 'good', or morality (1989: 3).

5. There are exceptions. Some, such as Gillett (1999), have sought to explore the implications of Dennett's work for social theorising. There are sure to be others. See also the discussion between Dennett and Rorty (both 1982).

6. This is part of Brubaker and Cooper's (2000), and Bendle's (2002) criticism of the use of identity. They argue that there is a theoretical inconsistency in a notion that is both super-fluid and static. They have a point. Analyses of scholars who do not explain under what criteria or conditions people create static or fluid identities will likely have omitted a crucial aspect of their subject. How this dynamism is achieved in practice is a feature of this book's analysis, particularly Chapter 4.

7. MacIntyre's concept of character also supports Giddens (1991) and Berger and Luckmann who see the relative rigidities of traditional social stratification as excluding problems of identification in comparison to modernity, in that people in the past were likely to identify closely with their social role: people were very much what they objectively seemed ([1965] 1991: 184). Jenkins disagrees and argues that whilst our concern with identity may be new (because of the extreme uncertainty and social change that typifies modernity) the denial of 'the project of the self' to people in the past – who had their own concerns – is 'at least an overstatement' (1996: 9–10): though Giddens's position is perhaps more nuanced than Jenkins implies (Giddens 1991: 74–5).

8. Addressing these topics there is of course a large body of literature that has discussed identity. Various forms of so-called post-modernist gender, sexuality, ethnicity, class and other studies have drawn on contemporary radical psychoanalytic philosophies typified by the work of Derrida and Lacan. Somers (1994) and Hall (2000) have synthesised and translated some of the theoretical nuances of these works for broader audiences. Thus for instance, if the notion of *différance* (Derrida 2000) – which implies that identities are as much about what they are not as what they are – is a unique contribution, then these muscular philosophical contributions are relevant and useful. I remain bemused and unconvinced – but mostly bemused – by many of these post-modern concerns. Without going into detail, the endless deconstruction of concepts and terms only to end up using them anyway (but 'now in their detotalised or deconstructed forms, and no longer operating within the paradigm in which they were originally generated', Hall 2000: 15–16; see also Brubaker and Cooper who also feel that Hall's contribution has been 'sophisticated but opaque', 2000: 9) seems to me to be an exercise in intellectual body building (see also Alvesson 1995, for a general critique of post-modernism from an organisational studies perspective). I am not ultimately embarrassed to admit defeat in really understanding much of this work, and more aggressively, would be the first in the queue to offer these new emperors some clothes to put on.

9. Those that have contributed to the concept of self-identity include Erikson (1968) who used the term 'ego' identity and Strauss (1959), who used 'personal' identity (as does MacIntrye 1981: 203). Goffman used both 'personal' (but used this to denote a narrow aspect of identity; the publicly and readily available 'information' about the person) and 'ego' identity (1968).

10. If our task was theoretical one might use Burrell and Morgan's (1979) axes to plot these theoretical distinctions. For our purposes a more simplistic metaphorical characterisation is sufficient.

11. Failing to avoid this separation in writing about identity is the point at which authors tend to expend much energy criticising each other's work. Jenkins for example argues that the distinction between personal and social identity remains in Giddens's *Modernity and Self-*

identity (1996: 15). However, it is perhaps unfair to criticise too harshly given the extent to which the language we use to describe things structures our thinking. It takes time for new and better vocabularies to remove old ways of using words.

3. Relationships

Strangely for a story to be so minutely focused on just two individuals our main characters so far lack the substance they require if we are to get to know how Paul and John go about crafting their enterprising selves. We are in dire need of some life content stuff: we need a setting. This chapter begins a process that will see texture, depth and meaning added to the episodes and events of Paul and John's working lives. This first of four empirical chapters examines Paul and John's talk of their social relations and what this means for their self-identities and their sense of themselves as entrepreneurs.

In the process we will get to know Paul and John. We will also begin seeking meaning beyond what people say and do. This is an inherently speculative endeavour. The argument I make, anyone's argument, requires at least a small skip of faith. The verbal footprints their narratives have imprinted through my research are indistinct. They require analysis and the proper place for argument is bound up with the narratives, bound up with Paul and John's story.

COURTING: GETTING TO KNOW ONE ANOTHER

Paul and John first met when John became an employee of Harbourco. Paul had worked there for a number of years since his early twenties. Paul had earlier been keen to leave the middle-England town of Maltonbury; keen to leave parents and those school friends content to remain. He was following the same Whittington trail that I too had followed, to see if London streets were paved with gold. Slowly and ineluctably Paul saw his mere job take on the attributes and seriousness of a career. Without really ever making a decision he had chosen this type of work over the unknown of other never-to-be-known possible careers. His friends – budding journalists, artists, musicians and the like – all seemed more interesting. Paul pondered whether he should go to university and become more like them but he liked building 3D solutions in his mind to the port engineering problems he confronted. Paul was the one among his friends that bought the drinks. It seemed silly to throw away what he had just because it wasn't cool. Cool looked like hard work. John's arrival at Harbourco coincided with Paul's realisation that this was what he was going to be doing for much of his future.

Fresh with disappointment and frustration at the bureaucratic inertia of his previous position at a rubber corporation, John was keen to make an impact in his new job. He had got the position via an introduction arranged by his father. John felt he would fit in, felt he could make a difference at Harbourco; it was small enough to get things done. He had worked for some friends' entrepreneurial venture after he had finished college, and though it hadn't worked out with them – John had got fed up with the narrowness of the job – but he remembered the dynamism and enterprise fondly, especially since he had seen how stultifying corporations were.

Harbourco operated out of an office in West London: the not too distant river Thames a faint reminder of the water-bound nature of their work. John had returned to the city where he completed his engineering degree at Imperial College. This time round he had a wife, and a seriousness and determination about work: reflected perhaps in his too keen a desire to take on the look of middle-age. Paul still enjoyed being a man about town (not difficult when you looked like the film star Rupert Everett), but the earlier disregard for work was slowly replaced by longer relationships with girlfriends and a desire for self-fulfilment through work: there comes a time in every man's life … .

In the stories Paul and John tell about the formation of Fenderco these moments of meeting and getting to know each other whilst working at Harbourco are important. They have worked closely together for some twenty years. Their relationship is important: it can tell us a lot about who they are. Somehow their meeting crystallised and mobilised a growing interest in career and a desire for success. Their friendship emerged from working together and coalesced through the working practices developed in Harbourco. When John joined the firm in the mid-1980s he found in Paul a kindred spirit. John explained that whilst

> I was finding my feet, I didn't really know a lot about fenders. I knew a fair bit about rubber and what you could do with it and how you could process it, but I didn't know what made a good fender system versus what made a bad fender system. So I would spend a lot of time talking with Paul, and I found that very early on that Paul was a much better engineer than […] the Technical Director.

As their relationship developed they began to realise that their knowledge and skills complemented each other

> what Paul and I found was when we were going out to customers, if we went out as a pair, we had a very good rapport in a meeting. I could come on quite strong on the sales side and he could come on strong on the technical side and I don't know what it was but we just clicked quite well […]. We won quite a few good orders working together.

Their relationship wasn't simply a convenient happenstance that smoothed out work problems: it was something they noticed and talked about, a reflexive relationship. John said that the spark of their working relationship

was very apparent because we spent a lot of time in each other's offices, we had offices more or less next door to one another. He was running the drawing office and so on, I was spending a lot of time on the telephone, bringing these inquiries in and, I have got an inquiry: what the heck do I do with it? First thing is go and have a chat with Paul, and let's go through the problems, what can be done, he would see more of this than me, and I learnt a lot from him. Although I am an engineer – perhaps my engineering qualifications were a bit higher than Paul's – he is a far better engineer than me. He has just got the imagination, he can see, conceptualise and visualise things better than I can. But then I like the precision of getting everything down on paper, working out proposals, presenting it, winning the order, and so that is why we are compatible, not conflicting.

The narrative that John presents is of a working partnership that built up drawing on their respective strengths. John described their differing approaches as 'both equally valid ways of doing it, you know, but completely different. You add those two together and it makes quite a strong match'.

The basis for their relationship or at least in terms of the narratives used to describe and emplot it, was by no means solely operational and work focused. It went deeper too. Paul for instance emphasised the similarity between themselves and between their fathers: 'John and I have very similar backgrounds, same age, different personalities, but our family structures are the same. We're both from families of two sons. We're both the oldest, elder sons.' Paul used to talk of similarity of upbringing as a compatibility and friendship signifier. Continuing Paul made an explicit connection between their fathers' entrepreneurial attributes and their own

[Our] fathers are both dominant figures and both are creative. You know I always felt that I was going to do this one-day [run his own firm].
You always felt that?
Yeah, with my father doing it, [I wanted to] from early teenage. You know, as a teenager, there were trials and tribulations, but I was always impressed by him, and John was similarly always impressed by his father. His father is very similar to mine, they have both gone through bankruptcies or near bankruptcies: it's never quite worked.

This familial association with entrepreneurialism is nothing new. It is well known that many children follow in the entrepreneurial and self-employed footsteps of their parent (Kets de Vries 1977; Zimmer and Aldrich 1987). The important point for our investigation is how the narrative about their relationship is being used to create a sense of, in this case, Paul's entrepreneurial self-identity.

Paul's narrative hints at the 'evaluative criteria' ('a set of fundamental principles and values') he uses to emplot his self-identity (Somers 1994: 617). For Paul the themed or selectively appropriated story of John and himself having familial and attitudinal similarities tells of evaluative criteria by which he both evaluates and constructs the relational dimensions of his self-identity. In other words Paul is creating relational similarity and affinity, and boundaries for creating difference through narrative expression. Paul and John may be different in their personalities but the desire to run their own business, to push further for success and surmount the obstacles that stymied their fathers, is an endeavour and a narrative that unites them.

Out of this entrepreneurial and relational compatibility grew a friendship. They are certainly not friends in the sense that they are particularly intimate or especially sociable. They are a different type of person: the looks, the likes, the loves. In describing their relationship John for instance reflected that

> we don't spend a lot of time socialising together and I think that that is a good thing, [...] because otherwise you would just get on each other's tits. [...] Like with married life, you can't spend twenty-four hours a day with your spouse, and I couldn't spend twenty-four hours a day with Paul – he would probably drive me nuts. And I would him.

They did spend a great deal of time with each other, working and being away from home. Both Paul and John's wives variously described them as being married to each other or the business being like 'another wife'. Their talk of friendship is based on work and running a business together: male friendship tends to be focused on doing (Rubin 1985). John said in answer to a comment I made about whether they were best friends, 'No, we are good mates. We tend to socialise, but it means going up the pub talking work most of the time'.

After realising they worked together well and making friends at Harbourco the years went by and they found themselves increasingly exasperated by what they perceived were the limitations of their managers, Paul and John investigated the possibilities of starting their own fendering company. This first ultimately aborted entrepreneurial initiative was the result of a complex variety of context specific and more long-standing motivations. These included the generational antagonism felt against the two directors (the topic of Chapter 4); the realisation that they 'owned' many of the contacts with clients and were already doing much of the work required for running a fendering company; and, as was described above, they wished to surpass the entrepreneurialism of their fathers' flawed enterprises and a build successful and independent venture.

Another contributing factor to this initiative lay in the dynamic of Paul and John's relationship itself. In one conversation in the meeting room of the Fenderco office, where Paul was reflecting on their increasing disillusionment with working at Harbourco, he said

John is a similar age and I was becoming ambitious and John was extremely ambitious and we were similar as individuals. It became very competitive between one another and the friendship developed, but sadly the two directors were leaving it all to us. [They] left John and myself to do all the work, we felt like we were very ambitious and we could do it ourselves. We were in our late twenties and we founded this partnership that was a legal entity, and we called it CDL – clair de lune – which today is our moneybox company that holds the shares. You know, so we formed this sort of partnership [...]. We set out a legal agreement and we wrote to potential ... er ... business partners and competitor companies if you like ... we had in-principle agreements very quickly [...], but you know we were both a bit immature and didn't really have, you know ... [pause] ... in hindsight, you know, we probably wouldn't have made it work.

This premature entrepreneurial attempt was an important step in the story Paul and John tell about the formation of their friendship and the eventual formation of Fenderco. John said

Maybe it wasn't the right opportunity at the time, but somebody had the faith to say we could work with them and take this out into the market because we knew what we were doing and so on. So I suppose then the seed was sown for the, something for the future, although we let it just sit there dormant for a few years. [...] It is like once you pop the question you can't go back and un-pop the question. [...]. We were 'partners in crime'. [...] This is where we coined the phrase CDL, you see, we had to come [to the meetings] with a sort ..., or at least a pseudo company umbrella, let's make it sound like a company and so on and we hadn't set up a company or anything like that. So we decided to call it [...] CDL Industries [...]. CDL – clair de lune – moonlighting: it is all very corny but we were dealing with these French guys .... [...], our little joke.

A joke that is part of an important quest-like story about how they cemented their relationship and embarked on the journey that led them to start Fenderco. The above narrative suggests that they were destined to remain wedded to pursuing this ideal. The evaluative criteria that they use to construct their self-identity – which centres upon a constellation of entrepreneurially derived values and principles: the desire to strike out on their own, to be free and independent, to be enterprising, and so on – is locked together with the story of their relationship to each other; their relational narrative.

Though their attempt was aborted they saw where it was leading. They were committed to each other. They knew the courting was over.

A LONG HONEYMOON AND FINALLY SETTING UP HOME TOGETHER

Their self and relational narratives do not stop with the formation of Fenderco.

Both narratives are dynamic; it's an on-going story. The narrative arc of the company's birth, its subsequent, continuing and future development also forms part of Paul and John's stories.

Shortly after this abortive attempt to start their own firm Harbourco was bought out by a north European port industries corporation in the late 1980s. The basic structure and function of Harbourco (now renamed EuroPort UK) did not change a great deal although the market they operated in was larger and the managers were accountable to the parent EuroPort. Paul and John thought that this development would provide them with the space and opportunity they desired. Their managers were nearing retirement and regardless of how things might turn out in the UK office Paul and John's new relationships with the staff and managers of the corporate parent company and the staff from operations around the world, seemed to suggest that ahead of them lay opportunities galore. For the time being at least going it alone had lost its compulsive pull. As they tell it today though it was still inevitable that their enterprising day in the sun would come.

Paul, now married with a young family, finally took advantage of the new opportunities to escape the stultification he felt at EuroPort UK and took up a position starting a new EuroPort office developing new markets in Asia.

John continued to work at EuroPort UK, but their connections remained strong. They would talk on the phone and see each other occasionally; neither were strangers to the self-affirming tedium of business class. Both felt their entrepreneurial venture was still alive, lying dormant. Paul explained that after he left for Thailand 'John and I remained friends. I moved to Thailand and we often talked and discussed about how it was a shame we did not continue the CDL company.' John also visited Paul in Asia from time to time on business, and he said that

> Paul was now on his own. I was on my own. We still needed ideas. So we still spent a lot of time on the phone to one another. […]. [Paul] still carried on helping me, you know, long distance, on quite a few jobs, […]. So there was still a lot of communication there.

Eventually after five years events coalesced and their plans for an entrepreneurial venture stirred once again. More mature and knowledgeable, the time and circumstances were right to start their own company.

Actually starting Fenderco and the divorce from EuroPort was however far from straightforward. Both Paul and John had again become increasingly disillusioned with their managers: John with the old EuroPort UK managers who obstructively hung-on waiting for retirement, and Paul with the corporate managers who he felt often left him exposed and vulnerable when he needed their support.

The decisive moment of genesis and separation took place on a plane journey. As John explains

> I was getting a lot of flack from EuroPort. I was finding it frustrating because there was too much paper work, a lot of travel. I was a 'company man' [...]: being told all the time by EuroPort that we must do things this way, that way. [...] Paul had his problems in Thailand too. These were compounded finally by the fact that he got expelled from Thailand, because they [EuroPort] had not given him the right work permit. I was pretty fed up in the UK. They [EuroPort] decided that I was the best person to go out to Thailand. [...] [But] I was not going to step into Paul's shoes and I told them this: 'I am not [going], he is a friend, you should be doing everything you can, it is your fault he got kicked out, you should be doing everything you can to get him back in. [...].' They wanted me to actually go across on the same basis that he was on [that is without the proper work permit]. I said 'you have got to be joking'. [...]. But I did go out to temporarily look after Paul's office in Thailand and [before I went out there] Paul was back in the UK from Hong Kong where he had moved down to. We flew out together and Paul said 'this is ridiculous'. And it was that flight out from the UK that we cooked up these plans and then I, we agreed, you know, basically, let's get out [of EuroPort]. I was frustrated more than anything – Paul was really really fed up. I was very very frustrated. So we cooked up these plans and right, let's start again: let's look again at who we should talk to.

Their venture was on once again. This moment of entrepreneurial creation is a key episode in the story they tell of their relationship. This is a moment that was always meant to happen.

Paul and John secretly met with competitor firms Ausfend and FendercoEurope and negotiated a deal that saw them form Fenderco UK. Paul had been sacked during this period and John resigned from EuroPort.

Once the first Fenderco office became established (this was situated South West of London: they relocated to Maltonbury after their first year of trading) their relationship took on certain routines and attributes. Paul and John talk of how initially the new work context of Fenderco caused certain problems in relation to the division of labour and their relationship more generally. Paul and John had to re-establish the working relationship formed at Harbourco five years previously; a lot had happened, they had changed. As John noted

> In the early days of Fenderco, you know we were doing more or less exactly the same job, parallel working together on every single job which was good because we had never worked in that way before together, so it was a good learning ..., ... a good chance for us to learn even more about how each other worked. We had been apart for five years, [...], so we were a bit rusty – we still had to get to know each other again, and the working practices.

In getting to know each other again there is once more an implication of reflexivity in their relationship. John would have needed to ensure that everything was 'all right' (Giddens 1991: 91) between Paul and himself, through self-examination of his part in the relationship, to have been able to ascertain that they had removed the rust from the relationship.

This talk of getting used to each other again in a new work context also shows that their relational narrative depicts good and bad relational states: an evaluative criteria of relational success and failure. The narrative of their relationship is one of a dynamic quest-like journey towards a mutually re-enforcing harmony, balance and compatibility in the pursuit of their entrepreneurial project. This narrative is dynamic because trials and tribulations from inside (the search for their own mutual interpersonal equilibrium) and outside (the challenges faced by new entrant firms from market and regulatory environments) have to be overcome if the business is to prosper; and for Paul and John to feel self-fulfilled.

Paul and John talked of this early period of Fenderco being fraught with financial difficulty and business being slow coming in. This caused friction and argument between Paul and John. For John this early honeymoon period was

> like when you go through a rocky patch in a relationship, you can argue a bit. [...]. But things got better, you know. As the business got better those pressures came off and we found ourselves working far better together: beginning to gel. So I am sure that first year was partly competition from others and partly us still really learning how to work together.

Paul and John also made some mistakes that added to their financial problems. One of which related to a contractual oversight that led to a serious under-estimation of the job time and costs. Paul explained that

> We tended to take risks that we shouldn't, but we needed the business. [...] from the outset there was only the two of us that were here, actually sharing the mundane aspects of the administration: ordering, chasing and preparing drawings. We were both, I suppose, fighting for a role within the business and nobody wanted to come out the loser. It's probably why we got stung so early on. [...] we were competing against each other. Certainly the first year, because of the difficulties ... Because we were facing such heavy competition and the market was particularly poor that year. We were not performing well. We did not get orders for a long time. Any we did get we were lucky to have. It was touch and go: a fractious time between us.

Their relationship narrative is reflexively dynamic. The interaction between external forces, actually running the firm and the relational narratives used to describe and structure these events, show Paul and John in a constructive search for mutually supportive work identities: they emplot the variety of events into a coherent and purposeful narrative.

They had begun to settle into married life.

MARRIED LIFE AND EVERYDAY TROUBLES

The story so far has been one of an interpersonal journey towards balance and equilibrium. With the survival of the firm and growing success Paul and John 'clicked' once again, as they had back at Harbourco. Now established in Paul's childhood town of Maltonbury they were both laying strong and permanent foundations. Continuing success saw the eventual arrival of Mark and Will (and an office secretary, Joan, and a part-time casual draughtsman, Jack) who acted as office assistants dealing with the bread and butter sales and administrative work.

Mark and Will, both in their early twenties, were green and keen to learn and get involved. Mark was a fresh-faced, open and thoroughly pleasant young man. Will was more of a character with a strong local accent, ponytail and biker's clothes, worn as the badge of his non-conformist desires. When I started the research the four of them had worked together for a few years; they were a team, working hard, and socialising together in their local pub, The Grinning Cat. In conversation Mark and Will also talked about the manner in which Paul and John seemed especially compatible. Will said this when I asked him about their similarities and differences 'I have always seen Paul as a design man. John has been the salesman'. Similarly Mark said that they

> can work off each other. John can sort of benefit from Paul's technical know-how and problem solving ability and perhaps John probably goes [on with things] when Paul would probably let it [the job] go a little bit. So together the whole system is interlocked. I think I can say having been in the firm three years that they are totally different in every way that you can imagine. [...]. You know socially, the way they work, and all the rest of it. I think that is the core strength within the firm. You cover the whole spectrum. You know that John is very sales orientated on one hand and we maybe get a lot of the smaller jobs that Paul wouldn't be interested in pursuing. Paul perhaps takes the more measured approach, more prepared to take his time over the longer, gestation period: It could be the longest project in years!

Compatible but different: matched. As we will see later however Mark and Will also use a different relational narrative to describe Paul and John's relationship, one which places more emphasis on the differences and tension between Paul and John, and the control Paul and John exert over them.

After recounting their teething problems Paul and John continue their story of how business improved and how their division of labour eventually became more firmly routinised and established. But included in their narratives was talk of continuing tensions and the occasional spat. These conflicts were quickly resolved though. John noted for instance that

> we tolerate each other very well. [...] I think we are both pretty tolerant of each another [...]. We rarely get on each other nerves, but when we do we have a

big argument and by the evening it is usually fine. We don't let the sun go down on it.

Despite this their talk includes stories that show how disjunctive and contradictory events are emploted in their relational narratives. These contradictory and conflicting stories should not be seen as in some way the realities that contrast to the rhetoric; that clichéd mainstay of academic argumentation. They are not narratives that lay outside the themed plot. Rather in terms of how self-identity narratives are constructed and consolidated, they are events that lie towards the edge, peripheral and relegated to a less central position in the dominant narrative.

Any story that hangs together too well is one that might be difficult to believe. In selectively appropriating the events for their narratives the evaluative criteria that Paul and John use to construct a coherent relational narrative must allow for disjuncture and conflicting stories. There were occasions where Paul and John would talk of events and tensions even after the initial honeymoon difficulties of getting the company running and determining compatible work roles were overcome.

One issue which gave rise to ongoing tensions for instance, related to how they approached company finance. Paul's could be described as strategic, and less generously, intuitive. According to Paul, John on the other hand

> likes to look at the figures ... and I told him that we would make half-a-million profit this year and he denied it, and he'd been looking up the accounts and he got all excited last week because he got the first draft accounts and it's ... [pause] half a million pounds. [...]. He's actually been physically hiding money during the year and I said you must be wrong, you know ...
> *What, you mean hiding money from you in a paper sense?*
> In a paper sense. I mean he'd been putting money into accruals and using ... deliberately poor exchange rates ... you know. I have this big problem with John over this. It's a big contentious issue, 'cause, you know, I'd rather have precise figures [and] not stash some money away. [Pause]. Obviously the bank balance is very important as well ... [long pause], but if you can analyse your figures, you know, on a crude basis, based on business and the orders you have in hand, and a rough knowledge of what, and how long they will take to fulfil, you can make a crude assessment.

In a sense the above example of financial management simply reflects different approaches to running the company. But it is also an example of how conflict can emerge from even the most 'interlocked' relationship.

For John, Paul's tendency to vanish was often a cause for irritation. John said

> Oh, there are times when he vanishes. He just disappears out of the office. He says, 'right I am off to see Barry' and that was at nine in the morning and turns up at two

in the afternoon and he hasn't been at Barry's all the time, he probably has been down to [this city], probably been down to [that city] but you can't find the bugger.

Paul would also turn his mobile phone off when he disappeared, as he did when I accompanied him on a site visit. Paul's (and to a lesser extent John's) work involved travelling to and from meetings at sites around the UK. A few of the major long-term contracts were based on sites that were within a couple of hours' drive and Paul would occasionally visit these sites without any specific meetings having been pre-arranged. Paul liked to look at the structures being built; liked to visualise the engineering problems on site, to see and smell the sea; to see how the concrete, rubber and steel hung together.

From time to time mistakes were made which also created tensions, as my notes reveal a visit to Maltonbury when the atmosphere was particularly tense

> John had written an article in a trade magazine in which he had used a picture and a conversion chart he had taken whilst employed with EuroPort. Because [EuroPort] was keen to see Fenderco suffer (Paul had told me much over the preceding years about how they were out to crush him) they had taken out a summons. This caused Paul a lot of irritation over the weekend: he was not that communicative over the weekend. Deep thought. [...] Paul was really annoyed with John. I asked Paul if he had ever lost his temper with John, he said that he did 'sometimes'.

These are examples of the tensions in their relationship. Conflict is included in the relational narrative, not suppressed. Their dynamic relational narrative also includes events that describe their friendship as a bond in the sense of a connection *and* a constraint (Sennett 1981: 4). The example above also illustrates a well-known feature of dyadic relationships: that it is difficult to 'shift blame, obligation, and responsibilities upon an impersonal structure when a crisis occurs, action is called for, or a decision is to be made' (Becker and Hill Useem 1942: 14). Both Paul and John are clearly implicated in a crisis. The conflict has to be dealt with. Paul and John's relational narrative described the mutuality and compatibility but also the occasional transgressions where the constraints are breached.

What then do these relational narratives of friendship – the courting, the honeymoon and everyday routines, and the troubles – tell of Paul and John's sense of entrepreneurial self? What is the purpose of this causal emplotment of events into episodes? What can the selective appropriation of the 'infinite variety of events, experiences, characters, institutional promises and social factors' (Somers 1994: 617), through Paul and John's use of an entrepreneurially-based evaluative criteria, tell us about how they construct, consolidate and express their self-identities?

Giddens is helpful here when he suggests that modern friendship can be described as a 'pure relationship' (1991: 87). A crucial element of the pure relationship is the way in which it contrasts with traditional relationships. Giddens explains that a friend (modern friendship) 'is defined specifically as someone with whom one has a relationship unprompted by anything other than the rewards that that relationship provides' (ibid.: 90). The pure relationship lies outside, or 'free floating', the 'external conditions of social or economic life' (ibid.: 89).

Thus defined Paul and John's relationship is clearly not a 'pure' one. Their account is framed by occupation, contract and obligation. But it is friendship, relational empathy and compatibility that dominate. As my subtitles have been implying their relationship resembles a traditional marriage in Giddens's terms, in that marriage is based on a formal and informal contract, chiefly orientated towards economic considerations and integrated within a set of network and transaction relationships (1991: 89). Giddens has elaborated these distinctions elsewhere by arguing that 'fraternity – bonds that come from shared, and exclusive, male experience – is not the same as [the pure] friendship' (1992: 126). Paul and John's narrative of friendship equates to this notion of fraternity: all well and good.

However, our task is not to define *what* their relationship is. Rather it is to ascertain what their narrative describing it can tell us about how they construct, consolidate and express their self-identities.

Giddens's objective in emphasising the difference between traditional and more intimate modern relationships is for the sake of clarity regarding his argument about modernity and self-identity. He also acknowledges that the pure relationship is a 'prototypical' (1991: 6) construct and that in practice 'in many sectors of modern life traditional elements remain, although they are often fragmented and their hold over behaviour partial' (ibid.: 206). Consequently though modern friendship relations exhibit more intimacy and less instrumentality than traditional versions, it is not totally absent, especially in their fraternally based forms. Paul and John's relational narratives combine aspects of both traditional and modern relationships. There are therefore some aspects of the 'pure relationship' that can help illuminate how their relational narrative contributes to their self-identities.

Part of Giddens' argument for the emergence of the pure relationship relates to the way in which a desire for intimacy is set against the flow of the dominant impersonal social life in conditions of high modernity. Intimacy becomes a positive sanctuary: 'privacy makes possible [...] psychic satisfaction' which helps counter the increasingly organised and impersonal aspects of modern social life (1991: 94). Paine, argues something similar: friendship provides a '*refuge* from the glare of public life and its burden of institutional obligations' (1970: 151–2, emphasis in the original).

However, because Paul and John's relationship is described in terms of a friendship but is not a pure friendship in some crucial aspects, their relational narrative might be described as a *substitute* for intimacy: an ersatz intimacy. This is not to imply that Paul and John are using their relationship as an alternative to other intimacies in their lives. My own observations of these non-work social relations and the length of time that Paul and John spent at work, suggest that these other intimacies were under at least some strain (both Paul and John were now divorced).

The crucial point is this: the story they tell of their friendship provides some of the benefits of a pure relationship without the associated degree of real or authentic intimacy. Paul and John's relational narratives about each other are not the real answer to achieving intimacy and a refuge from the 'alienating effects of the development of large, impersonal organisations' (Giddens 1991: 94), but they do function.

The relational narrative they express about each other does two things: first and fairly straightforwardly their narrative provides a dynamic and reflexive arena for expressing, accessing and confirming the evaluative criteria of their self-identities: 'we still had to get to know each other again', 'we were both [...] fighting for a role within the business and nobody wanted to come out the loser', 'when we do have a big argument [...] by the evening it is usually fine, we don't let the sun go down on it'. Second it provides a positive and mutually supportive sanctuary or refuge from the impersonal forces of modernity: in Paul and John's words their mutually supportive friendship-narrative cushions them against the 'mundane aspects of the administration', and the pressures of 'heavy competition' and 'the market'. But this phrase 'the impersonal forces of modernity' is somehow too vague. What exactly does their refuge protect them from?

As well as presenting the individual with greater spheres of impersonality, modernity confronts individuals with a plurality of choices: how to be, how to act, who to be. For Paul and John as entrepreneurs this plurality certainly serves to enhance their creative options. However, the entrepreneur operates in a famously uncertain environment (Storey and Sykes 1996) and too wide a range of choices would likely get in the way of the incisive and quick decision-making needed to be enterprising. Thus, their relational narrative and the refuge it creates specifically serves to minimise, channel and cordon off the infinite and 'indefinite pluralism of expertise' that modern life presents to individuals (Giddens 1991: 195). In other words the refuge is needed to make action possible, to narrow the plurality of choices, to encourage trust and to bracket risk. As we shall see however this ersatz intimacy whilst functional comes at a price.

As well as Paul and John's relationship worked, it didn't stay as it was for long. The success of the company meant it wasn't long before Paul and John wanted to expand and grow. This meant starting a family.

STARTING A FAMILY: WHAT THE CHILDREN HAVE TO SAY

Paul and John's engagement with their employees, as Chapter 5 in particular will show, are fairly typical and represent a mix of fraternal and paternal forms of management control (Curran and Stanworth 1979). Our purpose here is to establish how Mark and Will's stories of their employers compare with Paul and John's, and to see how Paul and John incorporate their relations with Mark and Will into their own self-narratives.

Earlier in this chapter Mark and Will described how the owner-managers were a compatible unit: a partnership. They also talked more inclusively of how they were all part of a team. Will said

> It is a good team and we all have a good relationship. […]. If there is one person who is out of place then the company suffers, there is no disputing that. But we are all a damn good team. There are certain days when you think what a shit that was because of a problem, because it is quite difficult: because of the bosses. Well at the end of the day they are the bosses!

Mark and Will were under no illusions that work was why they were there, or that their relationships with Paul and John were chiefly work related. Will noted for instance that 'when I'm in this building [the Fenderco office], I got tasks to do'. But Mark and Will also enjoyed their socialising with John and Paul out of work; the drinking in the pub and the dinner parties at Paul's house.

Both Mark and Will noted differences in the way that Paul and John would talk in the pub in comparison to work. Mark for instance talked about how John behaved differently on 'pub nights'

> it tends to be one way traffic with John, if you are talking about work. Nevertheless, he doesn't treat it the same way that he does in the office. But on other matters he has a good time and he is a good laugh. [He talks about] laddish sort of stuff. Sport, but not work.

Will talked about how in the pub Mark and he would

> talk and listen to Paul more [than at work]. He's always there [in the pub], always talking, and you learn things. He'll tell you things about 'have you heard this and that', 'oh really ...', you know ... [pause]. It's a bit boring sometimes. […].[But] Mark and I listen to him – you're listening to someone who knows what he's talking about – listen to how to do a sale or how to design something, or how this fender system works on this [or that] particular dock. Paul comes across as being a sort of guy that knows a hell of a lot about everything […]. And he comes up with some very interesting stuff at times.

And Mark said of Paul and the pub that

> Paul and I share a similar sense of humour and I always get on well with Paul anyway. So in that respect it is great. But a few beers go down and you start maybe [with] what has happened in the office and at the end of the day there are tantrums and problems.

Thus the pub talk did not always necessarily ameliorate conflict. Mark and Will's relational narratives were also replete with criticism of their managers. Mark for instance said these things about John

> He is unpopular with most people that come into contact with him, in truth. Not because he is a horrible bloke, because he is not, but [it's] just his manner. He's not what people tag him for. [...] I get on with John but I am sure a lot of people can't. You have to take him as you find him really. But that is his competitive nature: bad manners, hugely patronising, bloody arrogant really.

Mark also said that Paul was

> Cock-sure to the point that you might say he is arrogant sometimes. I don't think he is, but he does come across as a little bit aloof. [It's] not because he thinks he is better than anyone else, I don't think. He is a thinker and that is where he gets his strength. You say something to him and he just walks off. His mind is not always on what you are saying. Most people love him to death really.

John confirmed this more distant relationship that Paul adopts at work when he described the way Mark and Will were managed

> I tend to work with both of them. But I work in a very different way with them than the way Paul does. Paul doesn't call on them quite so much, but when he does he says 'I want it done now', whereas I have perhaps the majority of their time, in overseeing what they are doing in general. Every now and again when Paul wants his bit he will just go in there and say 'do that for me now', and you know it is fine.

Will had similar views to Mark and felt that

> Paul's a kid. He's a really easy-going sort of guy. John isn't that easy going. Some days you come into work and John's the nicest bloke ever: he's nice and makes you coffee; 'thanks for that, that's really nice of you mate'; 'thanks for doing a good job on a drawing'; 'great job, nice job mate'. And then he can start shouting for no apparent reason.

Both Mark and Will complained of how at the office Paul and John could be distant and unhelpful. Will said this of Paul and John

> You will ask him [Paul] a question and he will just look at you. Typically he will

look at you and just give you a really filthy look and turn away from you and carry
on with his work. And you will say; 'Paul I have a problem and I need to ask a
question', and he will start to discuss it with you and then he will just forget what
you are talking about and just ignore you. In the office you will say; 'Paul, are you
at work?' and he will say 'yes' and just walk off. [...] whereas John although he is
a crabby old git sometimes, he will tell you what to do, he tries to make it his query
as well. Not like Paul. John's attitude is very workified and Paul's attitude is very
playified. So that is how I see it and that is how this company works. You have got
someone very strict in his ways and someone who isn't, but at the end of the day
they work very well as partners. [...]. Paul is really a big kid and basically as far as
I can see he has got something to do one day and then once he has done that he has
finished work for the day. Then it is party time and that is every Friday night. He
works hard all week. Friday night it is pub, back at his place for more drinks. [...]
John is different, a workaholic. [...] He doesn't let himself go as much as Paul does.
[...]. Now and again us junior staff we get a bit uptight about John's attitude and it
is very much if you have a problem, John is busy with something else. If you want
an answer to that problem you ask John and he doesn't take kindly to being asked.

These comments from Mark and Will show that in different ways both Paul
and John appear distant and self-absorbed at work. The narratives are not just
simple tales of managerial control and employee estrangement but of long
suffering friendly affection and admiration. Both Mark and Will feel the brunt
of the owner-managers' self-absorbed behaviour but express friendship and
affection nonetheless. What these narratives hint at in terms of Paul and John's
self-identities (their projections of sameness and difference; from each other,
from Mark and Will) is a willingness to socialise and engage with their
employees on affective terms. But the terms are mostly unilaterally and
unequally set by Paul and John and with a degree of self-regard that plays on
the affective sensibilities of their assistants.

This use of Mark and Will to provide an attentive and affectionate audience
(a substitute intimacy), especially by Paul who was 'always there' in the pub
can be seen more clearly when the narratives of distance and instrumentality
that Paul and John used to describe their assistants as employees is taken into
account.

For Paul, his relationship with his employees is part of a company strategy

the fundamentals of business are fairly boring and fairly obvious but there is a
relationship with all of the employees – virtually - with myself. I'm keen to
encourage greater loyalty. It's quite similar in a way to Richard Branson, who
surrounds himself with friends and relations and em he's [pause]…
Done rather well.
Done rather well.
[Laughter].

This related to the occasional dinner party at Paul's house and in particular
a weekend away during the Christmas period. The tab – line of credit – that

was kept at the pub for Friday nights was also likely part of this strategy, although attendance was also a more ad hoc aspect of Paul's social life too.

In the office Paul and John's narratives are occupational, instrumental and generally affectively distant, as a few examples will demonstrate. Much of Paul and John's talk about the assistants concerned their supposed lack of performance or development potential. Paul mentioned that Mark had originally been hired with a sales role in mind, but he said that 'Mark's been really loyal and I don't want to lose him but he could be replaced. [...] He's not aggressive enough.' And from my field notes,

> Paul told me that he wasn't happy about the amount of sick leave that Will was taking. [...]. For a sales role you need to be available. [...] Paul and John have to deal with [nuisance calls] when Will should be. [...]. Paul then moaned that Mark and Will could show more initiative. [...]. [...] they would never be able to take the company over, that was a 'pipe dream'.

And in an interview Paul said this about his attitude to his employees and staff management

> You obviously get round to pay rises and bonuses, but I don't think it's a bad idea to get rid of somebody very swiftly. [...] Mark thinks the company would collapse if he wasn't around. I mean that certainly isn't the case.
> *How do you deal with this? Having this reasonably sort of intimate, personal relationship [with your employees] and yet you are ...*
> Oh quite well. You'd be surprised. No matter how friendly you can be with someone, asking for money, a pay rise, ... is not easy [...]. I've done it, I've been there [as an employee] and I know how nervous and uncomfortable it feels. I know the answers to the questions and I'm ready for them. I also like to do it as an element of surprise, call them in and say, bang, that's what you're getting, no discussion!

The relational narratives of friendship in Fenderco see Paul and John successfully inculcating a family culture in the face of significant control-based and operational antagonism. Their own narratives however display an instrumentally based reserve, distance and indifference to the affective environment they have created.

What are the implications here for furthering our understanding of how Paul and John narratively create their entrepreneurial sense of self?

CONCLUSION

I have suggested that Paul and John's relational narratives provide an affective or emotional refuge which enables them to be effective entrepreneurs; and to realise and create an effective sense of self. This refuge also seemingly excludes Mark and Will whilst at the same time seeming to include them. The indifference and distance exhibited in their talk above shows that the sociability and intimacy that they (Paul in particular through his use of the pub) have created acts as a substitute intimacy: a functional facsimile.

These distant relational narratives are not particularly unusual for men. Giddens argues for instance that men are often unable to engage in intimacy 'as equals, [...] but they are well able to offer love and care to those inferior in power (women, children) or with whom they share an unstated rapport (buddies, member of a fraternity)' (1992: 131). For Giddens intimacy is thus a 'matter of emotional communication, [...] in a context of interpersonal equality' (ibid.: 130). Obviously, the relationship with Mark and Will is unequal and hence the persistence of unresolvable contradictions leading to tensions. It is not that Paul and John really want intimate relationships at work, but, if for no other reason, it is likely that the length of time spent at work (in the office, pub and elsewhere) means that some substitute is needed: it provides for a family atmosphere useful for control and maintaining order as well as a refuge that facilitates entrepreneurial decisiveness.

Their relational narratives can tell us yet more though. I am conscious that the following sociological and philosophical links and claims are perhaps a little in advance of the empirical elaboration they require. I mentioned that a small skip of faith would be, and is always, required. But I need to introduce the sense of Paul and John's self-identities as constructed from particular 'entrepreneurial' narratives. Their entrepreneurialism is narratively built on the manner in which Paul and John attempt to squeeze events and episodes and push their inherently and unavoidably 'dialogical' use of language and narratives into 'monological' expressions of self-creation (Taylor 1991: 33). What does this mean?

Taylor argues that the way in which self-identities are narratively formed represents an important and distinguishing feature of modernity. He emphasises the 'fundamentally *dialogical* character' of human life and argues that

> We become full human agents, capable of understanding ourselves, and hence of defining an identity, through our acquisition of rich human languages of expression. [...]. But we are inducted into these in exchange with others. No one acquires the languages needed for self-definition on their own. [ibid.: 33, emphasis above in the original]

The contemporary ideal of individualism however, he argues, stresses the desirability of a monological and independent creation of identity. Like Richard Sennett who feels it is wrong that individuals should be expected to be 'endlessly looking inside for a sense of fulfilment, as though the self were like a vast warehouse of gratification that one's social relations had kept one from exploring' (1981: 117–18), Taylor feels that an individualised notion of self-identification underestimates the 'place of the dialogical in human life' (1991: 34). Moreover he argues that the search for authenticity through 'self-centred and "narcissistic" modes of contemporary culture are manifestly inadequate' (ibid.: 35). That is, he argues that if we deny our ties to others, and deny that any demands beyond our own individual 'human desires or aspirations' are important, the way in which we 'opt for self-fulfilment' will be 'self-defeating' (ibid.). Paul and John are willing victims of this mode of contemporary culture, and like many in capitalist society they suffer from 'the illusion of atomistic self-sufficiency' (Rose 1996: 156).

The implications of this argument are that Paul and John will not be truly secure and free from anxiety, or truly an individual until they engaged with others through different narratives. Their current individualised engagement with others attempts to deny the need for a dialogical engagement in constructing and maintaining their self-identity.

This implies that there is something wrong or inadequate with their engagement with each other and others, their evaluative criteria and their self-identities. Aside from the arrogance of this proposition (derived from looking at the reality of Paul and John's lives through a glossy varnish of contemporary social theory), what I am suggesting is also straying into territory which social science traditionally avoids: that is, values and shoulds. The manner in which social science and the conclusions it makes secrete values is a large and philosophically complex topic but the assumption of value neutrality in the presentation of scientific knowledge is now widely recognised as, at least, a conceit (Gergen 1978: 1347; Giddens 1976: 135; Giddens 1993: 9; MacIntyre 1981: 78). Thus Taylor (1989; 1991) and others (MacIntyre 1981; Giddens 1991, 1992; Sennett 1981, 1998) *are* arguing that people and society are doing things wrong and should do them differently. Conceptual narratives are inherently value laden. This book is intended to provide some 'bodied stuff' on which their theoretical speculations can feed (Geertz 1973: 23).

However, putting aside these reflections until the concluding chapter, this chapter implies that Paul and John don't in some way engage with others. Outside work they have kin and partners. And they have friends. I am one of them. But this chapter has shown that the relational narratives they construct *are* limited, insular and monologically oriented. This relational insularity is achieved through the narratives they construct and maintain about their relationship to each other, which dominates the relational horizon. Paul and John's relational narratives necessarily deny engagement with others as equals. This does not mean that there is no engagement or that the inequalities mean the same if they are in the office or the pub. What it means is that the engagement is a substitute, an ersatz engagement, where the narrative protects and closets their self-identities from harm's way. The degree to which their

Fenderco project dominates and structures their lives, means that it makes sense for them to encourage an affective, sociable and family working environment. However, because of their entrepreneurial, individualised and self-absorbed work self-identity Paul and John are unable to engage in authentic relationships in that environment. Hence, both Paul and John's relational narratives about each other and of others, serve to underline their dominant sense of themselves as entrepreneurs.

And yet the selective appropriation and incorporation of disjunctive and contradictory events into the themed episodes of their narratives allow for the biographical stories they tell to have milestones, believable depth (to themselves and others) and a sense of a journey travelled: it allows for the relational narratives to be dynamic and successful. A key component of this narrative dynamism is the way in which Paul and John have used their generational antagonism against their former managers as a spur to starting their entrepreneurial venture. The next chapter sees us re-examine the events of Fenderco's formation and development through the self-identity narratives of generational relations.

4. Generations

Paul and John's decision to start their business, as they sat high in the sky on a plane to Asia, was born of immediate frustrations with their managers. Deeper, more naggingly pervasive reasons, based on a sense of inevitability that they *would* one day become entrepreneurs and that together they formed a strong invincible partnership, led to this moment. Frustrations with simply being employed and answering to others also permeate their narratives. If, as we have seen, the friendship narratives Paul and John use provide them with an outward mask of emotional engagement with which they can absorb and deflect potentially confusing and distracting commitments, then there are other narratives which supply the drive and desire to determine their own lives.

One of these resources is provided by the sense that they were part of a generation of young and dynamic engineer-managers that were destined to wrest control from the 'old farts' who managed the industry they worked in. As we shall see this narrative of generational identification wasn't used as a distant and stale founding story: a simple rhetorical prop. Their generational narrative was alive, kicking and well maintained. It continues to sustain their sense of entrepreneurialism.

Why would they need this continually manicured narrative support? Hadn't Paul and John achieved all they had wanted? Paul felt he had overcome the vindictive attempts of EuroPort to quash and stifle him. John felt finally that he controlled his own life. The atmosphere of paranoia that accompanied the faltering first steps of the company had dissipated. Surely they were as content as entrepreneurs ever get? Fenderco was succeeding. And yet, still they were beholden to others; still there were 'old men' to rail against, hemming them in.

Fenderco was the independent joint venture partner of a wide, complex (a better word would be 'fuzzy') constellation of economic activity: Paul tried to explain, but I never really understood the tangled contractual obligations between the various partners. Occasionally in my more paranoid moments I thought maybe he had something to hide. Maybe he did. That Paul employed his wife as a tax dodge, that there were other murky goings on within Fenderco that lie at the margins of my ability to disclose, to show if nothing else that Paul, like most of us, selects and shapes the stories he tells.

Much was clear though. The parent company Ausfend was based in Australia and supplied the extruded and moulded rubber sections and components and shipped them to Europe. Compared to Fenderco, FendercoEurope was the more established and larger company that took the major responsibility for coordinating and manufacturing the fender systems. Between them they supplied many of the world's ports with their products. Fenderco would subcontract the assembly and installation work using finished fendering products manufactured by FendercoEurope: Paul and John would often oversee the installation process, especially in the more complex and elaborate projects where further engineering design work was required, as the structure developed. Often their projects would take shape over many months in conjunction with the building of the new port structures.

Every year Paul and John would meet with the partner firms at the Annual General Meeting (AGM), which would normally take place at plush hotel conference facilities in the holiday resorts of Asia or Australia. At one of these meetings in Australia Paul and John had been expecting to have the success of their venture celebrated. They had left the bad times behind them, business was booming and they had even expanded and set up new companies extending the range of Fenderco's operations.

They were in for a surprise. Jurgen the managing director of FendercoEurope, someone that Paul and John were close to both commercially and personally and had known since their Harbourco days, having all 'grown up' together in the fendering industry, had warned that the 'bosses' would not be too pleased with the subsidiary companies Paul and John had formed. One of these companies Steel Applications (Jurgen was also a co-owner; I said it was fuzzy), supplemented the activities of Fenderco, effectively bringing assembly and installation in-house. Paul and John thought Jurgen was being Germanically overcautious as normal.

Of course he was right. The 'old men' were not happy. As the AGM progressed it became clear that they were not in the mood for celebrating. Though not explicit (no one wants to appear rude) the message was clear enough: the 'bosses' in Australia distrusted their young upstarts and felt that Paul and John would over-charge the parent firm and lose sight of their joint commitments: that's what they would do if they had the chance. That was business. You have to make a buck where you see it, don't you?

Paul spoke angrily of how the parent company was not pleased by Fenderco's diversification or apparently, its success. Paul said they 'were annoyed that Fenderco, rather than remaining a poky little outlying office was now worth more than Ausfend'. Paul referred to the parent company's managers as 'backward' and a lot of 'old fogies' and elaborated that 'these old men want to retire, they want to take their investments. They want control over it [the whole partnership], but they don't have that because of the entrepreneurial nature of the joint venture [Fenderco and FendecoEurope]'. The 'old fogies' didn't understand, how could they? They were part of a different and older generation. A generation who did business the old fashioned way: they still called each other Mr this and Mr that, using all the formalities and etiquette; it was all old school ties, a fondness for moribund and inefficient technologies, and, lets face it, they really didn't have the business nous that was needed to succeed in the modern world, did they? They were a generation that should move on or move out; they should let the young guns run the show.

At least this is what Paul and John's narratives of generational identification tell us. Generational tales of affiliation and antagonism and the use of cultural and artefactual narrative markers combine to produce a specifically entrepreneurial self-identity narrative. All this will become apparent. But what exactly is a generational narrative?

OF TIME, STORIES AND GENERATIONAL NARRATIVES

A generational narrative is of course one of a myriad possible ways of talking that might be used to construct a sense of self-identity, drawing upon temporally defined and situated resources. As such it is probably as well that we make some comments on how time and narrative self-identity relate.

That time and space are central 'resources for the social construction of identity' (Jenkins 1996: 27) is perhaps crushingly self-evident. A storied sense of self is inherently temporal: 'The past is an important resource upon which to draw in interpreting the here-and-now and in forecasting the future' (ibid.: 28). Margaret Somers feels that

> people are guided to act in certain ways, and not others on the basis of the *projections, expectations, and memories* derived from a multiplicity but ultimately limited repertoire of available social, public, and cultural narratives. [...] To make something understandable in the context of a narrative is to give it historicity and relationality. This works for us because when events are located in a temporal (however fleeting) and sequential plot we can then explain their relationship to other events. [1994: 614, 617 emphasis added]

A 'generational' narrative can be seen as a part of a 'set of fundamental principles and values' or 'hypergoods' which are used by individuals as 'evaluative criteria' in crafting their self-identities (Somers 1994: 617, following Taylor 1989). The notion of generations is a narrative means by which we conceive of our own and other's temporality or place in time, and use to make judgements about how to interact with others who are crafting or have crafted different identities.

Given this relationship between time and self-identity it is perhaps appropriate to say something of what else besides generations might count as a temporal narrative resource. Social status, roles and events are all assigned temporal significance. Strauss uses the social conventions of mourning, and the requirements of not mourning for too long or for too short a time, as an example of the ubiquity of temporality in social affairs. He writes that at any one time an individual may be engaging with, and experiencing many different 'temporal identities' (Strauss 1959: 126, 129). Periodicity (lifespan, seasons, days, lunchtime and so on, Lewis and Weigert 1981), temporal regularity, scheduling, calendars and private/public time are all important symbolic organising principles in social life or what Zerubavel has called the 'sociotemporal order' (1981: xii). The use of generational narratives, access to, and control over calendars, schedules, public/private time and so on, are all significant resources in the construction of self-identities. An example from the research illustrates the broader point.

Whilst interviewing Mark over lunch at his home – who lived a few minutes from the office and was in the habit of going home for lunch – we were interrupted by at least two phone calls from John who wanted to know some specific work-related information on one occasion, and towards the end of the interview, when Mark would be coming back to the office. As is elaborated in Chapter 5 Mark suggests that this type of interjection into private time and space was a common occurrence and was not necessarily unwelcome (Mark felt it showed that he was needed). In this incident both myself and Mark (in discussing the legitimacy of John in making the calls) and John (in actually making the calls), were arguably mobilising and rationalising time as a resource, and thus an object of our 'evaluative criteria' (Somers 1994): how time should or should not be used. By using time as a resource, to evaluate and respond to the actions of others, we were also projecting temporal identities. In other words the negotiation over what time should be used for tells something (it might not be particularly profound or central) about who we are and what we want.

There are then potentially many temporal identity resources that might provide insights and understanding. Even the narrative of this book is subject to decisions about representing time. The way I tell the story draws on and represents time in a myriad of ways; ways that reconstitute what really happened. But none are spoken with such force and regularity, and none seem to have the currency, that Paul and John's use of the notion of generations has in describing their entrepreneurial activities. They are readily adopted to explain their frustration at the present and in telling of the frustrations of the past; they are used to explain why and how they became entrepreneurs; they are used to associate with a virtual community of others like themselves; they are used to explain why the future will be different: they are multitasking narratives.

OUR GENERATION: AFFILIATION AND ANTAGONISM

For Paul and John to talk of being part of a generation they are obviously claiming to be part of something. A generation is a notoriously amorphous something and the 'thing' they are part of might be better conceived as participation in a 'community of practice' (Lave and Wenger 1991), which can be considered to exist amongst persons whose interaction effects 'mutual engagement, a negotiated enterprise, and a repertoire of negotiable resources accumulated over time' (Wenger 1998: 126). Generational talk conceived in this manner, are narrative resources. In their conversation Paul and John talk of being part of a group of port infrastructure industry professionals. For them this mutual engagement as a community is centred on an array of design, sales and business practices which contrast to the practices of the older generation: the 'old men' of Paul's ire. There is a desire by the younger generation to introduce more modern practices into the industry. The boundary of this 'community' is defined by Paul and John's previous work at Harbourco together with those outside who worked in similar occupational roles for client and ancillary firms with whom they had regular contact, via meetings, phone calls and the like.

Broader elements of this community can be seen in one conversation with Paul, who was explaining the different markets Fenderco operates within and the corruption they have to deal with in some countries. He continued by elaborating on the nature of the fendering and port infrastructure industry

> We are working in a little village really. We come across the same people all over the world. There are not many people building ports, while there are quite a few people, our database probably covers 60% of the people.
> *When you say you are meeting the same people all the time, when did you meet these people? Is this whilst you were working for [Harbourco]?*
> You meet people all over the world. Maybe some engineers are working in the Hong Kong office [of the Ausfend parent]. You bump into them. John and I go to quite a few seminars. It is a chance to meet up with old acquaintances.

This community is not imagined. The people that Paul and John encounter are met face-to-face, and the relationships are sustained, if not especially regular. In between the face-to-face meetings at conferences and the like, Paul, John, Mark and Will would share, often comic and lewd, e-mail messages. The relationships within the community are not simply made up of chance meetings: they allow 'for a circular flow of feeling among the participants' (Goffman 1972: 18).

For Paul and John the generational encounters within the community of practice resulted in antagonism between its older members and younger members. They were critical of the older members as managers and identified with younger members outside the firm who occupied similar roles to their own. In recounting their stories they stress the generational aspects of their identity as entrepreneurs: they highlight their entrepreneurial distinctiveness in relation to the older generation of business owners whom they worked for prior to forming their own small firm. Paul and John talk of 'growing-up together' with a generation of industry colleagues. They came to see themselves as being part of a generation of younger engineers/managers in the industry, a new guard that will replace the old, with a desire to replace outmoded business attitudes and management practices. At one point for example, John talked about his early days working as an engineer/salesman in the fendering industry with Paul, and commented that

> it was fun because most of the guys we were dealing with were younger engineer[/managers] about our age. We were getting more responsibility. They were getting more responsibility. We had the ability, the authority, ... the financial discretion to decide how much we were going to sell it for, what sort of profits we were going to make. Likewise, these guys that we had grown up with, if you like, ... a lot of them were now getting the discretion to spend more money.

From the early days of Paul and John's occupational socialisation they identified with others in different rubber and port-related organisations that had similar sales/design–engineering jobs. Throughout my conversations with Paul and John these developing contacts and relationships were described as a means by which they felt connected to the industry or in the term I am using, the community of practice. They – a disparate collection of individuals engaged in building a career – grew up together. Paul and John 'do not simply share assumptions of a background of experience. They also share a *sense* that other members of the same generation share similar background assumptions' (Corsten 1999: 258, emphasis in the original).

This collective sense is made explicit in the following statement by John, which highlights the relationship between senior and junior staff within the industry

> It [the 'old fashioned' way of doing business] is also the way that [our old managers] always used to work. It was the old school brigade and the generation of people they were dealing with was the generation of older [guys]. We were dealing with the much younger guys, the guys who were doing all the work. [...] Fewer of these guys [managers of the older generation] were around, they were beginning to retire or die or get promoted into [senior, non-operational] management roles where they were not in charge of engineering departments anymore: they were in a management position, so they had no influence on what was being done in the engineering department. Our influence was to those people that mattered.

John's comments show a generational alignment with the operational and hands-on roles of port engineering on one side and those more senior managers who are not engineer/managers any longer on the other. It is the job role and organisational position that creates the conditions for a sense of generational affinity. John also spoke in a way which shows an explicit recognition of how age and lifespan is related to generation and the community of practice

> The sixties/seventies generation has turned into the thirty-somethings; they have come of age. If you are too young, you do not have the sway with an older guy. If you are too old the younger guy maybe thinks you are an old fart or something, but if you are within these age bands as the seller and within this age band as the buyer, you know you have got a degree of compatibility. [...]. Most of the people that we are dealing with today are between late twenties and say, fifty. If they are over fifty they are more senior and they are not really involved in us anyone, if they are twenty-five or younger they have rarely got the authority to do. So it tends to be that age band – not exclusively but generally – that age band that we are dealing with, which is sort of the same age band as we are here.

With talk of 'coming of age' and 'age band' John is defining the community of practice through recourse to generational narrative resources. The wide range of ages being referred to clearly shows that in itself specific age does not determine affiliation within the community of practice in anything but a broad sense. However, that John's place (as well as Paul, Mark and Will; John's use of 'we' indicates the others too) within the community is being categorised by generational affiliations is clear. John is identifying himself with a group of others who share a similar temporally based identity in addition to simple occupational identification (which includes designers, purchasers, sales and project manager at both assistant and manager levels, in an array of co-related roles).

Paul and John perceive a commonality of practice, even if that practice is organisationally disparate. There is a collective sense of being part of a group of engineer/managers who have a stake in the industry, a sense therefore of 'mutual engagement' (Wenger 1998: 291). While those outside the firm may be closer to the periphery of the community of practice the effects of interacting with them were nonetheless described by Paul and John as an important influence on how they viewed their Harbourco managers.

SIGNS OF GENERATIONAL DIFFERENCE: ARTEFACTS AND CULTURE

Paul and John not only saw themselves as part of a community they also interpreted and made use of the cultural and socio-technical aspects of the community's 'shared repertoire of negotiable resources' (Wenger 1998: 153), as a palette on which to compose new self-representations, identities and practices. Paul and John use these narrative resources to differentiate themselves from the 'older' generation of managers for whom they worked, which entailed 'a formulation of "them" and "us"' (Parker 2000: 199). That differentiation was a crucial part of the process by which they came to define themselves as young gun entrepreneurs.

Paul and John articulate a narrative of redundancy for the past way of doing business and a sense of helping to effect changes in business culture. John for instance, in explaining why they were currently getting involved in partnering arrangements with some of their larger contracting companies, said that

> The eighties was aggression. The nineties is, if you like, reconciliation and discussion, negotiation, 'let's do it', let's use a bit of common sense here. Let's not kill each other in the process. Business can be fun or it can be nasty. Let's make it a bit more enjoyable and profitable for everyone.

Paul was often very scathing about certain types of firms that got involved in government sponsored initiatives and awards. This attitude also extended to the way in which the industry association gave out awards at conferences for excellent design and engineering work. Part of this wry irritation related to the way in which 'the post war generation business managers in Britain tend to have the grand title of Chairman of Manufacturing when the company has two or three people': there was something distinctly fusty about this way of doing business. Similarly John compared his earlier employment under the old guard at Harbourco to his perception of business being 'old fashioned' in contemporary Ireland

> I imagine that must have been like business years ago when [our managers] started up [Harbourco]. There was very much a protocol which you had to follow and business etiquette, and these [are] … all broken these days. Things would work very old fashioned, slow, very laborious. [There was a] formality to business. [Now], rather than addressing somebody as Mr. all the time … you are calling them by their first names. And I think this is all to do with the advent of fax and e-mail and things like this, everything is much more informal.

More concretely in relation to his work at Harbourco, Paul 'became more and more disillusioned with them [Harbourco's managers]' because of the way that 'technology was moving on' and the way the 'market was changing'. Similarly Paul also said that

> There was always a certain amount of chaos within the company and they [the Harbourco managers] under-performed. Half the letters they were sending out to potential customers [were] apologising for not sending the quote they should have sent two months ago. And this went on and on. So, there were a lot of aspects of the company that I really was not impressed with although I liked the people.

Paul and John perceive, both in general and specifically in relation to their Harbourco managers, the now superseded generation of business managers as living in a culturally different business world. It was a world where the right social background was as important, if not more important, than professional management.

Paul and John's engagement with the cultural traditions of the industry, in a way that differentiated them from, and positioned them in opposition to the Harbourco managers is also evident in relation to their talk of socio-technical artefacts. This is not so surprising as 'the artefacts used within a cultural practice carry a substantial portion of that practice's heritage' (Lave and Wenger 1991: 101). To Paul and John new technologies were exciting, transparent and relevant. Paul and John felt that to the older generation these artefacts were opaque, invisible and irrelevant. In the eyes of Paul and John this engagement with socio-technical artefacts (such as the use of fax and e-mail) became emblematic of the perceived generational differences between the 'young' and 'old' managers. Today's sharing of an e-mail joke joins them to their community of practice.

There is nothing new in this emblematic use of objects and things. Each new generation meets things afresh and the advent of new things impacts upon generations differently. Karl Mannheim noted that when a new generation approaches a familiar problem, 'fresh contact (meeting something anew) always means a changed relationship of distance from the object and a novel approach in assimilating, using, and developing the proffered material' ([1928]1952: 293).

It is no surprise then to find that with the introduction of new technologies and novel business practices people will adopt different strategies of use and acceptance, as well as employ the new as emblematic of broader change processes. Clearly Paul and John align themselves with the new technology and identify the older technology with the older generation of business managers: the artefacts are an emblem of their distinctive entrepreneurial self-identity. In one conversation Paul spoke with sardonic amusement about the old technologies of business in Harbourco

> [there was the] telex, a machine which you used to type on a little tape and run it through and it was typed on a typewriter. I think by the eighties we'd got our first golf ball machine. Communications were slow, telephone systems were manual things where you used to pull little levers and connect to.

An important aspect of generational encounters is younger people coming into contact with the established cultural repertoire and using it to create new sets of meanings (Wenger 1998: 83). That process of mutual engagement around a socio-technical or cultural tradition plays a significant role in delimiting generational groupings within a community of practice. A key aspect of this engagement is the way in which the younger generation makes explicit aspects of the underlying assumptions of that tradition. As Mannheim notes one way in which past experience is incorporated into the present is through what he terms 'unconscious patterns' ([1928]1952: 295), which, using more recent conceptual frameworks, might be described as 'theories in use' (Argyris and Schon 1974, cited in Watson 1996: 325). Paul and John's account of their decision to break with Harbourco involved in part rendering into narratives the business and cultural practices – a bringing to the surface of the theories in use – of the previous generation of managers. It involved a conscious decision to substitute for these a new form of management practice through the establishment of Fenderco: an entrepreneurial venture.

GENERATIONAL ENCOUNTERS AND ENTREPRENEURIAL IDENTITY

A generational narrative supports their decision to start Fenderco. The narrative which emerged out of the generational encounters with their Harbourco managers continues to do good identity work, supporting a sense of themselves as entrepreneurs.

It's not easy setting up a fendering firm. There are many barriers to entry in the market and there are not many players. Despite Paul and John's narrative sense of inevitability that they would one day be entrepreneurs they were by no means destined to set up their own firm. Indeed the obstacles to so doing were large when compared to the alternative of remaining securely employed at EuroPort. One resource therefore that Paul and John drew upon in defining themselves as entrepreneurs, and acting accordingly, was their definition of their managers as members of an older generation. By juxtaposing themselves against the dull routine of the 'old farts' Paul and John also asserted their entrepreneurial self-identity. At one point Paul for instance, commented that 'when they [the two Harbourco managers] sold out, [the new parent company] thought they had just bought these two great entrepreneurs – the two managers. They had not realised there were a core of people beneath them'. Paul and John came to feel that it was they, not the two managers, who were the entrepreneurs. Throughout my time with Paul and John their talk was replete with the 'the will to conquer: the impulse to fight, to prove oneself superior to others' and 'the joy of creating, of getting things done' (Schumpeter [1934]1990: 133). Paul and John are both willing to take risks and create wealth: they both show an entrepreneurial identity.

If Paul and John had stuck out their frustrations at Harbourco/EuroPort it was likely that they would have succeeded and managed the firm. The buyout by EuroPort had perhaps come a little early for them. Their managers remained and were increasingly perceived by Paul and John as obstacles to developing the company into new markets that were emerging as a result of the recent merger. Paul and John were also disappointed and frustrated at the lack of ambition from the managers who they regarded as having sold out (literally and figuratively), and were irritated at doing the managers' jobs but not receiving the appropriate recognition or rewards. This is shown in a comment from John

> We had a few ructions and arguments with the management within EuroPort [both locally and in Europe], and we started trying to stretch our wings and flex our muscles a bit more. And it worked, and it didn't. Some of it backed fired on us, because we realised that [Name, local old EuroPort manager] was just spending all his time down the pub. And you were looking at the orders coming in and ninety percent of them, *ninety percent* of the business of that company, were being generated by Paul and myself. We realised that we were worth a lot of money to this company because we were making a lot of profit, and we knew that that profit was coming from us: that we were winning! We had this frankly not very competent technical director and the other ten percent were ones which were more or less people ringing up and saying they would like to order, so they did not have to do anything for it. [Name, other old EuroPort manger] by this time was looking more to spending time on his on boat and maximising his pension fund and how can [he could] you get out of this [the opportunities provided by the new merger].

There was little reticence or immaturity now. John was confident of their ability to create wealth and to do it off their own backs. Their sense of mastery is juxtaposed against an increasingly frustrated and antagonistic relationship with their managers, both locally, but also from the corporate leadership in Europe. To use a generational narrative in this way 'is to comment on the inabilities of others just as it celebrates the expertise of self' (Parker 2000: 204). Generation was a resource that they drew upon, reflexively and narratively, in processes of identification that led ultimately to the creation of Fenderco.

To a certain extent the owner-managers were pushed into creating their own firm by what Shapero and Sokol (1982: 80) term job-related negative displacements: their feeling of exploitation, dissatisfaction at what they perceived as poor management and a clash of aspirations for the future of the business. Certainly this sense of rupture in breaking with EuroPort is present in the talk of Paul and John. For instance, John talked about how one of the local EuroPort managers 'was really an obstacle for progressing things [their careers and business success] any further: [voicing the EuroPort manager's objections and his own reply] "Oh no, we have always done it that way". "[Manager's name], you have to change if you want to win more business".'

Despite these antagonisms the relationship between these young guns and the 'old farts' was not entirely dominated by conflict and binary opposition. It is not just generational antagonism but also continuity (learning from the 'older' generation) that typifies relationships over time within communities of practice (Lave and Wenger 1991: 115). A significant element of continuity associated with mutual engagement in practice and learning from the older generation was intertwined with these negative experiences. Both Paul and John acknowledged that they learnt from their previous managers. For instance Paul said that they 'taught us how the whole financial mechanisms of running companies worked'. Similarly they had respect for their managers as indicated by Paul's remark that 'we could have gone to another company and got a job, but ... it would have been disloyal ... [so] the right choice was to set up our own business'.

By bringing the process of self-identity consolidation into view one can capture the positive and incremental aspects of the social context of the decision by Paul and John to establish Fenderco: the sense of learning, but also being stifled by existing practices and the lack of opportunities. This tension is an example of the simultaneous construction of identity as sameness *and* difference (Jenkins 1996: 3–4). But it is also more specifically analogous to the double bind of the apprentice, as described by Lave and Wenger (1991: 115), where there is a contradiction between the need to engage with existing practice in the community (continuity), but at the same time have a stake in the development of that practice (change). Paul and John were keen to challenge traditional interpretations of business practice in their industry and offer alternatives. Specifically Fenderco espoused a sophisticated design and technology ethos and a higher degree of service orientation than was common in their industry. In one conversation for example, Paul described how 'The market is becoming increasingly technologically sophisticated. Ports are having to use specialists fendering firms. Gone are the days of just using old tyres for fenders. What we [Fenderco] offer that's different, is eloquence, better design and more cost effectiveness, where there is better down stream maintenance effectiveness'. This ethos represented a distinctive shift away from the business practices of the older generation.

At the beginning of this chapter I showed that this generational narrative is not just the stale and distant story of Fenderco's foundation. It continues to drive Paul and John and their generation to bigger and greater things. It continues to drive the antagonism against the old men. The talk of the Australian 'old men' and their lack of entrepreneurial understanding repeats Paul's oppositional attitude to his previous managers at Harbourco and EuroPort: the generational antagonism (justified in entrepreneurial terms) remains a prevalent feature, serving to maintain his entrepreneurial self-identity in the face of corporate control.

And the sense of community is likely to continue. The narrative resource may change but identification based on generational difference is an enduring feature of their narratives, even to the extent that John recognises that he will one day likely become an 'old man' himself: 'I am sure the time will come for us when all the people we are dealing with are far too senior to have any bearing on our type of work, in which case we will have other people coming up to fill that role.' One day John won't not only understand the e-mail jokes, he won't be willing or able to access the technology.

CONCLUSION

The three features of these tales, generational affiliation and antagonism, culture/artefacts and entrepreneurial identity, constitute a micro-examination of a 'particular' temporal narrative resource. The generational narratives that are presented in this chapter have two key effects for Paul and John. First, in their account it acted as a catalyst for the decision to embark on entrepreneurial careers by setting up a new venture (that is self-identification as 'entrepreneur' predated what Shapero and Sokol term the 'entrepreneurial event', 1982: 76). Second, the narrative of generational difference along with other narratives, sustained them in the transition from securely employed professionals to risk-taking creators of a new entrant firm: and the narrative continued to sustain their entrepreneurial identities even when the original generational opposition was made redundant or replaced through their starting Fenderco.

At the beginning of this chapter I suggested that this discussion would elaborate and position these generational tales within the broader temporal narratives of self-identity construction. In the previous chapter I showed how Paul and John's work relationships were one-way emotionally guarded affairs geared to protecting and facilitating entrepreneurial initiative. In seeming contrast, this chapter has described the use of narrative resources in a community of practice where a coherent but essentially occupational and 'generational' identification binds a disparate group together. However, whilst the sense of community shows a dialogic engagement, there are two ways in which the generational narratives complement rather than contradict the previous chapter's conclusions.

First, to my mind Paul and John's talk of generations is about 'replacement'; for them the past is not being repeated, and the future is being projected on the back of their project, Fenderco. Thus, despite the – albeit disparate and limited – continuity implied in their community of practice, the atomistic stance enacted and adopted through their relational narratives is shared with their generational narratives. Their narratives are, to borrow a concept from Richard Sennett (1998), discontinuously reinvented. There is in other words, a purposeful sense of a dislocation from the past created through the narratives, and hence an attempt to limit the well springs of their self-creation to an insular and self-referring set of temporal relations.

This use of generational narratives is not that surprising or particular to Paul and John. Traditionally however the churn of generations has been regarded as a process of rediscovery and renewal of 'modes of life' (Giddens 1991: 146). Shifts in the spatiality and other contexts of modern life have meant that it is our relationship to our own lifespan and not a generation (in Giddens's 'real' sense, and not as it has been used here) which provides a central focus of temporality to our self-identities. This means that the relationships that Paul, John, myself and you the reader, make with others 'have to be mobilised through the reflexive ordering of the lifespan as a discrete and internally referential phenomenon' (ibid.: 147–8). Talk of generations is a narrative aspect of that 'reflexive ordering' and an element in the narrative production of a biography (ibid.: 53–4).

What this means to the current analysis is that the narrative of generations becomes not one of renewal, rediscovery and reliving, but a narrative of *replacement*. Because talk of generations *is* still being used, it is obviously because it is 'reflexively justifiable' (ibid.: 146) in the production of self-identity. In a similar way to the previous chapter, Paul and John use generational narratives to bracket themselves off from a set of relationships (those of the 'old men') to enable and protect their sense of entrepreneurial difference. This chapter has shown how this is accomplished at Fenderco.

A second pervasive feature of their narratives is their 'oppositional' nature. Paul and John use a generational narrative in a similar manner to the concept of labelling, in that the creation of an opposition or deviant group of others, a group that needs replacing, also helps to create and define the individual (Becker 1963). Alternatively their use of generational narrative might be seen in a less binary manner using Davies and Harré's concept of 'positioning', 'whereby selves are located in conversations as observably and subjectively coherent participants in jointly produced story lines' (1991: 48; see also Czarniawska 1998: 41). For Paul and John their labelling or positioning articulations about generational relationships provides a vocabulary, a 'negative identity' (Kärreman and Alvesson 2001: 84), with which to identify their sense of difference and sameness in the pursuit of their project. For Paul and John though, it is a particular and emphasised identification against others that feeds their self-conceptions, and as we shall see in Chapter 6 there are other narrative themes which also draw on oppositional narratives. Again the focus on opposition and difference implies a monological orientation rather than a desire to engage with others dialogically.

These broader aspects of identity and the similarities and differences between the empirical chapters will of course be explored further in the concluding chapter. For now enough has been written to achieve the main purpose of this chapter: to provide an example of how the temporality of self-identity is narratively produced. Throughout this chapter the concern has been to show that Paul and John used the generational encounters with the 'older' generation as an important self-identity resource in thinking of themselves as entrepreneurs. Those encounters in turn were influenced by Paul and John's encounters with younger engineer/managers in the wider industry; with whom they developed a sense of affiliation or in Mannheim's terms, a generational 'consciousness' ([1928]1952: 290). This affiliation is closely related to recognition of similar job roles, organisational–hierarchical positions and career paths. However, this affiliation went beyond the functionality of similarity: they came to regard themselves as part of a generation, not just a transorganisational occupational grouping. In the process of self-definition Paul and John utilised the cultural repertoire of the community of practice manifest in business culture and cultural artefacts, as a resource with which to construct new meanings – new attitudes towards business, a sense of the new replacing the old, a sense of replacing and opposing the past, a sense of themselves as entrepreneurs.

5. Space

There is a tendency to take for granted where things happen. For the managers and employees of Fenderco work takes place in offices and factories, but it also happens whilst socialising in pubs, in the home and at conference locations around the world. Self-identity narratives provide coherence to these different spatial regions. In the previous chapter we saw that generational narratives give shape to a broad spatially diverse community of practice. As we saw this coherence is not seamless, and in this chapter I unpick the way Paul, John and the others' narratives are constructed in the places they work and play.

Initial expectations of the fieldwork envisioned me spending most of my time at the Fenderco office, though broader vistas were also inherent to the original research design (Down 1999a). In practice I found it difficult to hang out there. It was often a claustrophobic, tense, industrious and quiet place. There was only so much sitting around, photocopying, using the computer and everyday banter one can engage in as a researcher, before you realise that you're being a nuisance: interrupting the everyday flow of events you are there to capture in the first place. At least this is how it is in a small firm with an open plan office. So my research spilled over seamlessly into other aspects of Paul and John's work and social lives.

Without these different spaces a truncated and impoverished picture – the *wrong* picture – would have resulted. Paul and John do the business of being entrepreneurs, and of being managers, salesmen, engineers and designers, in a variety of places. The social interaction in the office, pub and so on produces different narratives: of control; of playing with roles; of self-construction and experimentation at the boundaries between different spaces; and yet more control, of self and others.

Let's look at these different spaces and the self-identity narratives they produce.

SCENE ONE: THE OFFICE

The office. Difficult not to picture it in some form or other: open plan; computers; photocopiers; manila files; staplers; hole-punchers; bulging shelves; piles of drawings; bigger piles of paper; strange bits of rubber and steel (samples? paperweights?); scale models of fendering products; framed certificates; coffee mugs. As we know from the television series *The Office*, the noise of small unfathomable machines, whirring and shushing, evokes an atmosphere of friendly familiarity and purposefulness. Fenderco's offices were the same. And yet every office is different. They are peopled; they figure in narratives.

Towards the end of my time in Fenderco the interior layout of the office underwent a renovation. Prior to this the rented premises very much had the feel of the converted farm sheds they in fact were, and the set-up could best be described as adequate. Paul and John were keen to develop the office so that they both had a semi-private office space and that overall it projected a more professional image. Paul mentioned that it was not good for a company that espoused an image of aesthetic dynamism and innovative design to have such a dowdy office. Aside from the laminated flooring and the new paint, the revised layout included two glass partitions which now surrounded Paul and John's personal workspace. In a phrase redolent with panoptic themes to excite the Foucaldian scholar these transformations of the internal office space became known as the 'goldfish bowls'.

The new layout seemed to be of particular interest to Mark and Will, though there was also a general sense of excitement at how the renovations represented a coming of age for the company, which would hopefully solve some of the company's 'people' problems. Interviewing Mark at his home late on in the fieldwork he explained that even after the installation of the goldfish bowls 'most of the time I would say that the office atmosphere is perhaps tense; probably because of John. He is a bit of a control freak. He likes to be in earshot of everything that is being said and done'. Surprisingly perhaps John himself confirmed this, as my field notes show

> Whilst waiting in the reception/holding area at [a Ministry of Defence port], John was talking about the office layout in Maltonbury. He said that he likes to listen out to what's going on. He said that he doesn't trust the others. He keeps an 'open door'. He stressed that this was about teamwork. Often when Will or Mark was on the phone, John would pass a note to them.

When I asked if Paul was different in this regard Mark replied

> Not particularly because sometimes Paul is one of the people that makes it difficult as well. Everyone has bad days. I certainly have bad days. They [Paul and John] are taking the brunt of the responsibilities in the firm and the rest of it. Some days John will snap at somebody and everybody will hear because it is a small office. So someone will get a lot of pasting [and] it sort of sets the trend for the day otherwise. You have got to think, right, steer clear of John or Paul when they are in a bad mood.

Mark further commented that John's behaviour 'has its benefits and sometimes he will hear something, pass a note or something, and come and help you out of something you may have dropped yourself in. But on the other hand I feel he would be better to let people get on with it'.

Mark then talked about the future development of manager/employee relations after the renovations and the newly installed goldfish bowl offices were bedded-in more 'Hopefully, with the new offices you can take yourself away and sit down and discuss it. I still think that you should discuss it rather than have a slanging match'.

The 'tense' (it was also described as 'claustrophobic') atmosphere occasionally flares up in the form of the owner-managers 'snapping' at the staff. 'Slanging matches', altercations and 'bollockings' were a common feature of life in the office. On one particular occasion Mark described how he 'had trouble with John' about a disorganised file

> We had a little purchase order for somebody. The file was swinging around on top of one of the files behind me and then one morning John had it [the file] and said 'it was all in a complete mess and there was no order in there at all'. He sort of went mental at me, and I said 'well I haven't touched the file for about four weeks'. So I had a look through it and all the stuff was actually in there. He just kind of looked at it and decided it was everyone else's fault. So I went back and threw it on the desk and said 'it is in there if you want to look'. You know we had a bit of an argument and I accused him of treating us like children and said it was about time he stopped doing it. [...] He said 'Oh, I have upset you'. Too right you have upset me and I told him as well. On that particular day there it hadn't been justified. Just the general way he handled the situation shouting and bawling in front of everyone else.

What is particularly apparent in these comments and the experience of this workspace more generally is the constant degree of co-presence. One is reminded of Sennett's characterisation of how the intimacy of open plan offices can tyrannise: 'people are more sociable, the more they have some tangible barriers between then' (1974: 15). The overall impression – seen too in Chapter 3 – is of constraint and suppression. Simple spatial tightness of co-presence seemed to give little room for much more than work and pressured antagonism.

Not much sense of an 'entrepreneurial' identity in the office then, and this absence of entrepreneurial activity (creativity, innovation, dynamism) was explicitly recognised: Paul would talk of getting his creative ideas whilst driving, at home or visiting ports and sites in situ. John talked of work being most 'fun' when he was out on site trying to make a sale. Aspects of Paul and John's *entrepreneurial* self-identities were absent in the office. Or, given that their entrepreneurialism obviously structured and informed all their work activities, was at least not formed, consolidated or maintained there through everyday practice. Their self-identity narratives as employers and managers were more apparent in the office. The office space was a disciplinary space, a space of control.

Though there was also a lot of 'hard work' and 'fun' to be had in the office, much of it centred around mildly scatological humorous faxes and e-mails from industry colleagues in their community of practice, it is obvious from the above descriptions of the tensions, intensity of co-presence and constraints often apparent that other spaces would figure in the accomplishment of work, social relations and self-identities in Fenderco. Spaces are not monolithic in their demands on role and identity; boundaries are fluid and overlapping. It is to those other spaces that I now turn.

SCENE TWO: THE SITE

When Paul and John visited the ports and harbours for meetings about the progress of projects they became different people. I too would also enter a different world when accompanying them on these trips. Suited and tied, I would become a Fenderco employee for the day, or on another site visit where Paul did not feel it necessary to hide my researcher status, I became what I in fact was: a researcher. Even being this besuited, professional and 'business school' researcher felt strange. In Maltonbury I was a researcher but I was also myself, on site I became someone else, something novel, something a little grander.

It should not have been surprising to find that Paul and John changed as well. When visiting and talking with the personnel from larger contractors Paul and John would often become deferential. This change was largely due to a *conscious* and acknowledged shift from being themselves as entrepreneurs and owner-managers of a successful small business, to playing a role of small contractors in large projects within corporate management structures.

One of these visits involved Paul and I driving for a few hours and visiting a very large site where Fenderco were installing fendering equipment for a series of large locks. The visit included a variety of meetings, a lot of waiting around, and a tour of the site: partly for my benefit and for Paul to see the progress of the project. Whilst the various meetings with the representative of the sub-contractor were relaxed and informal, my field notes explain that the more formal meeting with the corporate project managers showed Paul in a light I had not previously seen. Various specific technical issues arose in the meeting and Paul was asked in an obviously leading manner if he had considered the full implications of his design. One of the corporate project managers also tried to affix some blame (and thus the cost) to the failure of some equipment to Fenderco, but the sub-contractor defended Paul on this issue. Throughout the meeting, as my notes show

Paul's general attitude here was conciliatory and perhaps a little obsequious. This is interesting because John did this too [in another visit]. Paul was not so grand. Similar to John at [the other site] he was a small player in a big game here. Afterwards in the car Paul said that this was about 'pleasing the customer' and that it was a definite business/personal strategy. In the car on the way back Paul said that the superior attitude of the [name of corporation] guy was nothing to what had gone before and Paul has had to take a bollocking from him before; but you just take it, its good business.

The fluidity with which Paul is able to engage with the role of subservient small contractor without bringing his dominant sense of himself under threat is spatially interesting. It is suggestive of Collinson's observation that 'within the power inequalities of organisations, identity is constantly open and available to be negotiated and re-negotiated, defined and re-defined' (1992: 31). Paul is able to play the subordinate without losing his sense of security or stable sense of self, by redefining his subservient and potentially undermining behaviour as 'good business', and therefore contributing to the successful narrative expression of his main work self-identity. In other words Paul acknowledges that the role he is playing is not really him. Paul in this case accepted the definition of the situation by the dominant contractor, whilst justifying it in terms of self-interest.

A similar change took place to the way that John presented himself on site. At the end of a technical progress meeting regarding Fenderco's minor role in a large defence port contract he tried to make a sales pitch about how Fenderco's new Steel Applications products might be used. This did not meet with much interest though the major contractor suggested that he 'might be able to sneak in on' some work with another sub-contractor down the corridor. This swiftly brought the meeting to a close and John had an impromptu meeting with this sub-contractor, whilst myself, and John's main site contact stood by. As my field notes reveal

John then went to see the [sub-contractor] guy about the steel structures (ladders, gates, walkways and so on). Introductions were made and the impromptu meeting was very sharp and pithy. John stood up. The other guy sat down [...]. After some initial description, what we do type stuff, [the sub-contractor] asked very directly what you [Fenderco] can do for us (about 2–3 minutes into the chat). John 'sold' the company and arranged to be sent tender documents. Interesting to see this, it was definitely a sales pitch. John was quite stressy and hyped up.

Though in this case John was not especially subservient, the short amount of time that the sub-contractor allowed him to talk meant that John spoke with a nervy air of keenness. He spoke in a way which said that his company was there to serve, in a way that is typical of the sales situation and of John's general sense of Fenderco being a service orientated business. Again I was surprised by the change from his normal self-assured and entrepreneurial self in Maltonbury.

These are fairly impressionistic observations but they were nevertheless strikingly obvious ones. In each example Paul and John became different people. It is perhaps not coincidental nor is it surprising that this occurs away from the main site of Fenderco's activities. It may also be one of the reasons why Mark and Will did not go on site very much.

When asked about whether he went on site Mark answered

> Virtually never. But I don't really need to, although one thing from the future point of view that annoys me a little bit is that I don't want to be totally office bound forever. I mean just to be able to look at the premises of a supplier or go to a site, you know it'd be great, because I feel a sense of pride. It sounds a bit cheesy but [pause] ... I mean you have a sense of pride, something to work on.

I have no clear evidence to suggest that part of the reason why Mark and Will did not go to sites and conferences was because of Paul and John's apprehension of self-identity disclosure. But the sites Paul and John visit certainly produce a different identity dynamic, and Mark and Will's absence was particularly pointed. These trips from Will and Mark's viewpoint look like exciting privileges. For Paul and John the project sites are a necessity and on occasion require them to recast their self-narratives through the adoption of certain potentially threatening roles. These non-entrepreneurial small contractor narratives were however, unsurprisingly, told in a way (that is, by explicit acknowledgement in Paul's case of the talk being no more than role playing) that reinforced rather than undermined their central entrepreneurial narrative: the pivotal narrative of the Fenderco locale.[1] It is to other spaces of that locale, the homes and pubs that Paul, John, Mark and Will used, that I now turn.

SCENE THREE: THE HOME

Paul lived in the centre of Maltonbury, close to both the office and The Grinning Cat pub. Paul's home was special. Not just because it was a magnificent building, but also because for Paul, the others and me, it was so clearly a boundary space between work and play. The house, which Paul's children referred to as the 'castle house', is a large and old (the foundations date from the 16th century) town house located next to the Catholic church, and up until more recent times was a nunnery. Paul and his partner rented the property cheaply given its size and location as a result of being interviewed, vetted and deemed suitable tenants by the church offices.

Inside and out, the stonework, the decor, oak floors and panelling looked as if it was from a *Homes and Gardens* feature. It was all so impossibly and stylishly old and slightly decrepit. Dinner table talk of renovations always conjured up the image of the Forth Bridge. Whilst the planned for projects were slowly accomplished, mostly by Paul's partner (though I contributed on one occasion, helping to build a sandpit for the children in the garden), there were occasionally unplanned and disastrous events such as when the water pipes burst, flooding the ground floor and basement, which flattened aspirations for a while.

I would usually stay at the 'castle house' on my visits to Maltonbury and being a large house in the centre of town, it saw much toing and froing and a variety of social gatherings. These would often include John, Mark and Will: as Will indicated 'we're always invited out to things and parties, we all go out at the weekend [...] all the time, we're sort of just a group of friends'. These friendships also extended to dinner parties at Paul's home.

At one of these weekend parties with other friends from London and Maltonbury present, Mark (also the brother of Paul's sister-in-law[2]) and Paul told derogatory stories about John and his management of home life. My memory of this and my field notes reveal that I was surprised (I wrote that I was 'quite shocked') by the tone and personal nature of these stories and the mutual candour displayed by Mark and Paul. Surprised both in a general sense, but especially because of the blurring and playing with work and social identities that Mark as an employee, and Paul as an employer, were engaging in within this boundary space. And this was more than the jokey office joshing that they all engaged in. I can only assume that Paul expected Mark to understand the implications of the back region location (that is, disclosure) and that they would not broach the subject elsewhere.[3]

Another example of how Paul's home was used can be seen in how Will would sometimes stay the night at Paul's rather than drive home on his motorbike when he had had too much to drink. Will explained that there was an understanding that he always had a bed for the night as long as he didn't 'intrude'

> I'll stop at Paul place. What happens basically is that you go there [the pub] for a quick pint and if the mood is right a quick pint turns into six or seven quick pints. [Laughs]
> *[Laughs], Right.*
> And then you've just got to say look, well usually what you do is after about two [pints] or, well in the old days, after about two or three, you said 'look I've had enough of drink now, can I stop at your place?' and that was the time when you decide you'll have a drink or not. 'Yes', ok, 'no', your not. Paul's sort of always said to me in as many ways if you ever need a bed 'Will, there's a bedroom there for ya'. [...] Obviously you got a watch, [pause] you can't always intrude because they have got people, guests round and that. But strictly speaking the house is there for me to use, just the bed really. [...] You know [I] got straight into the house, went

to the bedroom, eight o'clock in the morning, got someone, got Paul banging on the door, time to go to work today.

Towards the end of the research period though, Will began to stay over with Mark, who had bought a house near to the office. Continuing the conversation I asked

Is that a regular thing, or?
Not as regular now, no, we use to be, well it sort of ..., you felt you were doing it regularly but you were doing it once every two months, you know, perhaps sometimes twice a month, then you wouldn't do it for ages, it just felt that sometimes maybe that you were putting people out.

There are then some limits to the use of Paul's home. Will ultimately preferred to stay out of it given the choice between a back region influenced by his employer, compared to one based on the mutual work identities of a colleague. For Will it seems there is, despite the apparent blurring of identities, as Bourdieu has written, a 'tacit acceptance of one's place, a sense of limits [...] or [...] a sense of distance, to be marked and kept' (1985: 728).

These examples are perhaps inconclusive in terms of the narratives that are being used. We get the sense of Paul's house an occasional and incidental boundary space. The pub however was far more central to their identity projects.

SCENE FOUR: THE PUB

The Grinning Cat pub is situated, like Paul's house, in the centre of Maltonbury, and it takes ten minutes to walk to Fenderco's office from the pub. The pub is a free house and has a quality restaurant and a beer garden. Its clientele is varied age-wise but generally middle-class, professional with some who are employed (or under-employed) in various creative pursuits. Compared to the other pubs it has a cosy, middle-class, old-fashioned feel, and for Maltonbury at least, is a bit trendy. It was a very regular venue for most of the people at Fenderco and Paul kept a 'tab' (line of credit) at the bar, which would often pick up the cost of most of Friday night's drinking.

Pubs are typically seen as socially open areas where individuals from different social backgrounds and of varying ages meet freely and forget their differences (Hunt and Satterlee 1986: 65–6). This is something entirely different from the experience of The Grinning Cat as Paul and John used it. The examples below show how they experimented and explored differing identity narratives, whilst nevertheless maintaining the dominant employer-based control which they exported from the office region. The forgetting of identity differences were not entirely possible for Paul, John, Will and Mark, although the differences inherent in their social relations were presented and engaged with in the pub as if they were equals. As will become apparent, the boundary region of the pub, where work and leisure identities intermingle, create interesting tensions between front and back regions of self-identity.

Act I: Office Talk in the Pub

Paul and John were frequently away from the office so meeting in the pub on Friday evening was a convenient way to catch up with the week's events. Though everyone kept in contact via mobile phones, there was unsurprisingly, given the human desire for co-presence (Boden and Molotch 1994), a perceived need to talk things over face to face. Indeed even if they had been in the office most of the week, there was often an informal debriefing and discussion of business at a more general level. Friday night was in many respects a ritual and the evenings in The Grinning Cat served many different purposes for all involved. Work was just one aspect. This multiplicity was reflected in my academic interest as well. In a conversation with Will for instance, I ventured:

> *I'm quite interested in the Pub, this Friday night 'institution' where I've ... I've been there [interrupted] ...*
> You've been there on *many* occasions. Pissed as a fart as well! [Laughs]
> *[Laughs] Unfortunately not with a tape recorder, because that would always be quite interesting, but I've made a few notes myself. [Pause] I mean how does that fit in with all the Fenderco office stuff?*
> When I sit down on a Friday night in the pub it's basically: 'good week at work lads', couple of pints, wind down. That [is] typically what it should be. Obviously what happens sometimes you get up there and there's a bit more than an average amount of drinking takes place, particularly between myself and Paul. And we have a good argument about ... [pause]. We argue and we argue ...

The use of the pub for work was not universally appreciated however. For instance Will, though acknowledging the pub as a good place for an 'unwinding session' also felt that

> [...] the problem you get a lot of the time is that you get a lot of work talk, shop talk, and you do get times when you think I've hear all this shit for the past 50 hours this week, before we get pissed. [pause] Lets talk about shagging birds!
> [Laughter]
> Let's talk about my new car or my motorbike or something else, or let's talk about the price of butter. And then you try and make a bloody conversation, and that leads you to the arguments, you know it's not worth it at the end of the day. So Mark and I tend to talk about bikes, booze ... [pause]. Obviously we'd never go up to their [Paul and John] conversation about work and say 'how do you do this [job]?', or

'how's that [job] going on?', you know. But I suppose really it's a time we can really get together in the early part of the evening; we can have a sort of debrief as it were. How the week's gone, what we have all done. Because no one knows what I've done, really.

There was a hierarchical dynamic to evenings in the pub, with business discussions taking an early priority over more general socialising. In addition, as Will implies when he says that he would not interrupt if Paul and John were talking business, the early evenings in the pub are often used for 'strategic planning' discussions, as well as entertaining the occasional business visitor. John for instance commented that

we maybe go down the pub rather too much but really that's really just to catch up, because he [Paul] is busy during the day and I am busy during the day. How do you get the chance to share ideas and talk about strategy and so on? It's best to do it outside the office.

Thus, most of the time the pub was perhaps a more comfortable place of work for Paul and John than it was for the assistants. However, the annoyance felt by Mark and Will at work talk taking too much time away from socialising, suggests that rather than a strict demarcation between front and back talk, there is a degree of 'argument' and negotiation about what is discussed. When it is noted that wives, girlfriends, friends (myself included), acquaintances and other visitors (both business and friends) also frequented the pub (and often Paul's home) on Friday and other evenings, the pub can be seen as a place of fluid, overlapping and clashing narratives, where different identities meet and develop.

Act II: Control and Portable Identities

Despite a nascent proceduralisation of human resource issues at Fenderco, much of the 'career development' and many other personnel management tasks, such as discipline and control, are more ad hoc in nature and location. Moreover, given the degree to which all of the core work group are busy at the office during official work time, and the extent to which they engage in 'slanging matches' through the day (though these also continue and re-emerge in the pub, as the talk of 'arguments' above suggests), it is perhaps not surprising that staff management extends into the pub.

On one occasion, Mark was thought to have made a costly mistake. In my field notes I described the situation

The incident involved Mark forgetting to send some documents which meant, ultimately, that some parts did not fit together on site, the mistake cost the company around £5,000. Paul lost his temper at the time, and Paul explained that he was keen to show his employees that it was their responsibility: 'to make him sweat and learn'.

Later Mark, still maintaining that he was not responsible for the mistake (as it turned out he was mostly right), received the softer part of the 'bollocking' at the pub. And though, as Mark said later in an interview that 'It was a big issue between me and Paul for a few days' he also implied that this use of the pub was fairly 'normal'. Thus, the ostensibly private back region of the pub is used here as an explicit site of management control: Paul effectively defines it as a front region where authentic self-identity is covered up (Giddens 1984: 126) by the cloak of an employer and managerial identity. For Paul situating the 'bollocking' in the back region of the pub demonstrates his ability in exporting the power inherent in his management role beyond office workspace. It also suggests that this aspect of Paul's work self-identity is relatively portable, especially compared to the spatially restricted, more performed identities that we saw when he was on site.

For Mark however there seems to be little escape, and the convivial and public nature of the pub environment means that he must act reasonably. Paradoxically in this example the pub becomes a front region in the sense that activities in it are on view and public, in contrast to the privacy (although this was not private from the others in the office) that accompanied the earlier 'bollocking' at the office. This aspect of the incident reflects what Bourdieu has also noted: the capacity to 'make public' is a key aspect of social power, including 'all forms of benediction or malediction, eulogy, praise, congratulations, compliments, or insults, *reproaches*, *criticisms*, accusations, slanders' (1985: 729, emphasis added). In this example the pub can be both front and back region, and the employer and managerial objective ('the bollocking') is enhanced through the indeterminate nature of the identity work that is taking place: Paul is using and controlling the spatial regions of the Fenderco locale through an expansive managerial self-identity.

Another example further demonstrates the control which Paul and John have exported from the office. When first hired, Will initially misconstrued the freedom of the post-work pub nights. Will noted that after an initial period of being 'in the shadows' at the pub after being taken on

> I would get really plastered and make a complete twat of myself. It got to the point where Paul said, 'Look Will I think you better just keep to yourself, because we've got customers here. [...]. On that occasion you may have pushed it a bit too far and we don't want to see it any more'. And from that conversation, right, it's been agreed all round, between myself and John and Paul, that I have really calmed down, me and Paul still have the occasional *discussion*, not argument anymore, it's talking, it's discussing.

In this Will may be seen as taking time to learn how to behave appropriately in the pub as a place of work, where Paul and John entertain business visitors. His actions initially following the rules of the social setting (the pub as a back region of sociability and mutual disclosure) rather than the pub as an extension of Fenderco's office. Both these examples are redolent of the 'spatial practice' of Lefebvre, who argues that individuals are often required to develop 'spatial competence and performance' (1994: 38). In this case Will's abilities are initially lacking, but through explicit control and experience, Will's work identity as a Fenderco employee became more fluent (that is, competent) as he engaged over time in the various spatial regions of the Fenderco locale.

Act III: Pubs, Piss-ups and Punch-ups – the Limits of Portability

The behaviour in the pub would often get quite loud and rowdy as alcohol flowed and people let off steam in a mostly good-natured sort of way, facilitated by company credit. There were often bouts of mock verbal abuse.[4] On one occasion for instance Will, in response to Paul's mock demand for compliance over some issue or other (but also possibly because I was there and Will wanted to show off in some way), put two fingers up and said 'up yours, it's not work now, you tosser'. Paul then play acted the role of the manager and said, 'Right, you're fired'. Will explained later in an interview: 'You have a few beers, you're really excited, it's the weekend, and you just don't give a shit what you say really'. Both assistant and owner-manager were happy to indulge each other in a parody of the manager/subordinate roles.

Even my role as a researcher would be included in this parodying. Will would sometimes for instance, bait me with comments such as 'What do you fucking academics know about the "real" world?' My rough and ready responses to these comments would seek to both legitimise the role of researcher and for good measure I would remind him of my previous experience with the 'real' world of work. Both of us knew we were playing with our roles: all of us recognising that we were not defined by them.

The spatiality of this parodying talk is not incidental but rather a manifestation of the change from front office space to a boundary space. Despite the pub being a space where Paul and John import aspects of employer and management control, it is also a site where other broader and more fixed social identities, such as roles, figure in the relationships between managed and managers. These colliding identities and roles exhibit contradiction, ambiguity, and produce parody and play-acting behaviours and the exploration of the limits and boundaries of their respective self-identities. Though this mocking behaviour is also exhibited in the office surrounding it is more explicit and combative in the pub.

One minor example demonstrates the point. Early one Friday evening in the pub I was talking with the four of them about cars and stuff and I recalled an earlier conversation with Paul and John that day about how company profits were good now and that they were thinking of buying new more luxurious company cars. In my field notes I noted the following about what was said: 'In the pub a loose word from me (whoops!) about John buying a new Porsche Boxer from profits this year, caused some joking from Mark and Will and some very slight mock embarrassment from Paul and John'. In itself neither my blunder nor the substance of the talk was especially important. But the joking from Mark and Will about how they 'slaved away', whilst Paul and John spent the profits, and the exaggerated embarrassment at being found out from Paul and John, illustrates the broader and more fixed social identities (in this case a cartoon role characterisation of moneybags entrepreneurs verses down-trodden workers) with which they experimented and played. This type of mocking behaviour also occasionally resulted in some extreme behaviour.

Will was talking about his relationship with Paul and how one Friday evening they had this big argument

One night [...] I think I really pissed him off. He ended up on the floor one night, when I went home from the pub.
You threw him on the floor?!
No he threw me on the floor [Laughs].
Oh right [Laughs].
But it was just a scuffle: [quoting his and Paul's earlier argument] 'I was right', 'no, *I* was right', 'NO! *I* WAS RIGHT!', ... and then I wrote on a piece of paper 'I resign', and he said 'I'll keep that piece of paper until Monday'. So on the way out I thought I'd get it out of his back pocket and bin it: this writing. What happened was that I went for his back pocket, unbeknownst to him, and he just turned round and grabbed me, I insisted on going back and we were going back and eventually I just fell on the floor. And er, I er ... thought, Christ! [Laughs].
[Laughs].
And I felt really bad about what had happened, and I thought well, that's my fault what went on there, that shouldn't have happened, and on Monday morning he was in a real strop with me. So I went in and I have walked in [the office] and he says 'I want to talk to you about Friday night'. And I thought oh no.
Did you think here's the job gone then?
Here comes a written warn ..., not a written warning because it doesn't happen here [in Fenderco], but here comes Mr big bollocking time. And he never said anything to me.
What he didn't talk to you?
He didn't talk to me that day. And I must admit I'd actually sustained really quite a badly bruised shoulder after I gone into the wall. I mean he did push me: it was the way he pushed me or something, I don't know ...
This was about half ten at night?
Totally bladdered. [Then later that week] Paul come up to me and said 'I'm sorry about what happened the other night, I shouldn't have done that, but what has happened [was] because of my living in Thailand. Pick-pockets are about at that particular time [at night] and for some reason I thought I was being pick-pocketed' – it's a really daft excuse – [reporting Paul's speech again] 'I'm really sorry to have

hurt ya', he said, 'but I'm sorry'. And that was it. Nothing more was said. There's been the odd joke, people like John, [reporting John's speech] 'trying to ...' (John was there at the time) 'been beating people up again as usual, Will'. [Laughs]. *[Laughs].*

Among the many noticeable aspects of this dramatic incident is the way in which more sober (in both senses!) front region behaviour seemed to emerge in the office. Paul was likely embarrassed about the whole thing (which is probably signified by my intuitively *not* asking him about this particular incident). In the pub the employment contract inscribed on a scrap of paper became the humorous indicator of their respective work identities. In the office playing with their work identities had for Paul at least, become an embarrassing indication of the potential consequences of sailing too close to the back regions in the ambiguous context of the pub environment. This is an extreme event to be sure, and in more than one sense an identity boundary was (almost) breached.

These examples – chosen to illustrate both the extremes and the general flavour of the Friday nights in the pub, although there were also quieter nights, especially when one or other of them were absent – are also suggestive of Goffman's notion of role distance, which Cohen and Taylor describe as 'ways of commenting upon a role while playing it' (1992: 2). Both Paul and John and the assistants made ironic plays of their roles. As was noted in Chapter 2 however, social roles such as employers, managers, entrepreneurs are not synonymous with self-identity. Whilst Will might have the role of a Fenderco or small firm employee and sales/engineer assistant, he brought far more into his encounters. As MacIntyre writes: 'The beliefs that he has in his mind and heart are one thing; the beliefs that his role expresses and presupposes are quite another' (1981: 28). Thus the examples show people with self-identities playing 'with' their perceived roles, demonstrating to each other that there is far more going on if one takes a trip outside the office.

CONCLUSION

I have shown that the work of creating a work identity for Paul and John has a spatial characteristic: they consolidate and bring coherence to their sense of self through reforming their narratives to suit the various locations they inhabit. That different spaces create different identities cannot be in doubt. But we can be more specific.

First, we saw that boundary spaces such as homes and pubs can be places where engagement with contradictory situations, encounters and roles can potentially undermine central self-narratives. In everyday social practice however, the threat of having to adopt potentially undermining narratives is easily dealt with through explicit and conscious playing of the role and thus incorporation within the central narrative.

Second, not only does the shape and layout of the office have a bearing on the social relations of control and hierarchy, but it also provides a frame to how self-identity is crafted in that space. The degree of co-presence and other self-identity expectations create a constraint on the form and variety of self-identity expressions. Paul and John are themselves constrained into reproducing managerial identities in the office, as well as benefiting from the control across boundaries which their 'rank' (Goffman 1971: 65) as employer/managers brings.

Third, Paul's home and The Grinning Cat provide spaces in which to experiment with other roles and identity narratives that combine, through incorporation into a central biographical narrative, into a sense of who they are. However, the employer/management control objectives of the office are not escaped in the pub (neither for Paul and John, or more obviously Mark and Will). Indeed, the control of the office is simply exported by Paul and John into the pub. Paul and John seek to, and in fact do ensure that they are in control of themselves and others. Through their control of the spatial regions of the Fenderco locale they reassure themselves and consolidate their self-identity as employers: through their identification of themselves as employers in those regions they differentiate themselves from others that share those spaces.

There is though 'a complicated nexus of possible relations between meaning, norms and power' (Giddens 1984: 126) between the different regions. Paul and John's control of these spaces is not omnipotent. The examples discussed above show that new and varied self-identity expectations also emerge and proliferate for all involved, in addition to the overall picture of employer/manager dominance.

The above summary is not a sufficiently expansive discussion, and a few points of elaboration are needed. It is worth suggesting that if the pub can be described as providing a stage for role distancing behaviour, then part of what this behaviour is intent upon is actors mutually exploring and expressing a variety of self-identities. Cohen and Taylor write, for example, of how groups create '*activity enclaves* in which people try to dig out, through hobbies, sex, games, sport, a safe place for self expression and identity work' (1992: 114–15, original emphasis). Since our group does not comprise members of equal status and consequently the rules and norms of both the office and pub spaces can be in conflict, there is a sense in which the pub is not a 'safe place'. There is more ambiguity and negotiation than in the office or on site, but the control brought to the pub by Paul and John nevertheless pervades and frames the extent of the activity. However, as Ackroyd and Thompson add, these enclaves also 'have their own distinct characteristics' and 'are not simply the result of the forces surrounding and opposing them, but represent an emergent social context which serves as a significant "identity site" in its own right' (1999: 55). This suggests that it would be wrong to see the use of the pub solely as an adjunct of other locations.

Another point of analysis should also be more speculatively and briefly explored. The exploration and expression of identity work is also apparent in the obvious enjoyment of the repartee in the pub and home. Many of the above stories suggest that people enjoy playing with each other's narratives. Will in particular relished getting close to the edge in relation to what was allowed by Paul and John. The discussion has in one way or another woven its way around notions of boundary, edge, line and margin. Sennett suggests that it is at the edges of social interaction that social identities emerge: that 'the edge is a zone of engagement' (2000: 178). He argues that 'an identity, [...], takes form through the social interaction of people at the edges of their personae, those boundary negotiations between self and other' (ibid.: 186). Thus, the actions and interactions observed in the pub and elsewhere, in this sense, might be described as constituting the edges of managerial and play space, where the some of the identities of explicit managerial power blur and combine with the mutual but unequal exploration and expression of identity work in Paul's home and the pub.

Discussion of role constraints on identity, of course, raises other issues about the disciplinary nature of organisational life. This chapter has shown that the office space taken in isolation would produce a claustrophobic, 'confined', 'enclosed', perhaps an overbearing disciplinary space (Giddens 1984: 145). This is not an insignificant conclusion for research into small organisations given that it suggests that in some work settings at least, research which methodologically restricts its purview to the workspace, would likely produce representations which overly discipline work identities (Reveley et al. 2004). This chapter has also shown that other regions provide a partial and limited respite from disciplinary hegemony. Like Giddens – who, favouring Goffman's analysis (1961), argues that Foucault erroneously uses the disciplinary power of the particular ('the total institution') to describe society's nature in general (Giddens 1984: 155) – this chapter shows that despite the disciplinary nature of modern social and organisational life, the self-identity making activities of human agency are in fact more varied in their practical engagement with different spatial locales.

Paul and John's self-identity strategies and their Fenderco project might be described as an attempt to combine, socialise and control as many of the broader social systems as possible (that is social systems relating to leisure and work), through their partial ability to control the spatial locales of their lives (Giddens 1984: 142–3). Paul and John may thus be engaged in an attempt to structure their lives through the creation of a coherent self-identity locale, against the spatially fragmenting tendencies of late modernity, based on their reflexive project of Fenderco. Thus Giddens writes that despite the decreasing importance of place and locality for the conduct of lives in modern societies, 'active attempts to re-embed the lifespan within a local milieu may be undertaken in various ways' (1991: 147). As with Paul and John's talk of generations, the regional expansiveness of the control Paul and John exact over the Fenderco locale, can be seen as a part of the way that individuals attempt to reconstruct traditional locality and spatial embeddedness in reflexive projects of the self (ibid. 206–7).

One final related comment should be made in anticipation of the theme of autonomy in Chapter 6, and in a reiteration of its discussion in Chapter 3. Sennett has argued that certain forces of modernity have created a shift towards people favouring the private and individual, over public and civic identities and roles. A consequence of this individualisation of society and the self, he argues, has been an incessant search for intimacy with others and a 'belief that real human relations are disclosures of personality to personality' (1974: 339). Therefore, because of the aforementioned tendency for co-presence and intimacy to tyrannise, he argues that people paradoxically, in the act of personal disclosure also shut out its possibility. The Fenderco locale is a stultifying and claustrophobic place to be: there is little room to escape. In the project of Fenderco Paul and John attempt to cast the various spaces of their locale, co-opting others such as Mark and Will, using the mould of their own employer and work-dominated identities. They are individualising their sense of place in the world. The attempt can only partially succeed because both the enormous spectrum of social systems and other's identities from other places intervene and 'resist', creating new hybrid identity regions. Paradoxically even in the Fenderco office where they ostensibly have the most control of their own and other's identities, the tyrannies of intimacy and identity expectations derived from other social systems deny the full realisation of their project. In other words Paul and John cannot shut out the world, or remake it in their own image.

NOTES

1. 'Locales refer to the use of space to provide the *settings* of interaction'. Thus, whilst locales are often synonymous with physically bounded entities such as a home, these settings for interaction can have 'a range of other properties specified by the modes of its utilisation in human activity' (Giddens 1984: 118, emphasis in the original).
2. Mark initially found out about the job by bumping into Paul next to the gym which is directly adjacent to the office and offers a discount for Fenderco staff. This use of geographical proximity and kinship in recruitment and selection procedures is common among small firms (Dick and Morgan 1987; Ram and Holliday 1993).
3. The reference here to 'back' and 'front' regions derives from Giddens' notion of regionalisation, where he – in an explicit criticism of, and divergence from, Goffman's early

work on front and back regions ([1959]1990: 109–40) – does not necessarily equate the back region with what is hidden away and more authentic, and vice versa. Giddens notes that if the front regions were no more than dramaturgical 'façades' then ontological security could not be sustained or achieved. Thus 'the differentiation between front and back regions by no means coincides with a division between the enclosure (covering up, hiding) of aspects of the self and their disclosure (revelation, divulgence). These two axes of regionalisation operate in a complicated nexus of possible relations between meaning, norms and power' (1984: 126). The use here and later reflects the definition of the situation by social actors rather than any spatially fixed notion of regionality: each space must be defined and negotiated by its inhabitants. In this case Paul and Mark are defining the space as a back region of disclosure.

4. Moule (1998) has referred to this type of behaviour as ritualised verbal resistance, and suggests that it may act as a social pressure valve in temporarily equalising unequal work relations.

6. Clichés

Previous themes, 'relationships', 'generations', 'space', of this book leapt into order even whilst I was in the field, and have maintained their boundaries more or less, through the data analysis, subsequent iterations and onto these pages. Doubt and confusion certainly informed the interpretation and analysis, but the clarity and obviousness of the themes seemed to form their own coherence. The theme of this chapter, 'clichés', was a little different.

There was something special, something unconvincing about the language Paul and John used when speaking about *being* entrepreneurial. I was struck by the familiarity of much of what Paul and John said: it seemed only to confirm, support and replicate what the literature had said about entrepreneurs, owner-managers, their employees and their ways of doings things. They seemed to be talking in just the same hackneyed way (as if they were saying lines from a script learned at some fictitious entrepreneurial school), as the owner-managers in other studies. Maybe this was what one was supposed to notice when researching entrepreneurs? Paul and John were entrepreneurs; of course they would talk this way. However it was, the cant of entrepreneurialism seemed to run deep in Fenderco, and I remained intrigued by how corny, how 'clichéd', Paul and John's talk often was.

The thought that there was something particularly interesting about 'their' way of talking kept nagging my mind. But for a time I simply consigned this irritant to the many other unresolved intellectual backwaters of the project: it simply wasn't an idea suited to any leaping. The notion of clichés kept coming back though, and I started to take it seriously and asked what effects their talk might have on their conception of self.

Immediately it should be clear that my application is an unapologetically analytical one. Paul and John don't recognise or actively narrate the concept, as they do with the notion of generations. Space and relationships are ubiquitous social narratives: conceptual organising devices for sure, but obvious and uncontentious ones. The theme of clichés is different. As such we require another type of conceptual leap to be confident in using it. In comparison to preceding chapters therefore a little more conceptual elaboration is needed before returning to look again at Fenderco.

UNDERSTANDING CLICHÉS AND THEIR SMOOTHING FUNCTION IN FORMING AN ENTREPRENEURIAL SELF-IDENTITY

Cliché is defined in the *Oxford English Dictionary* as 'a stereotyped expression, a commonplace phrase: also, a stereotyped character, style, and so on'. It further relates the word to its adjectival attributes as clichéd, 'hackneyed; characterized by clichés' (Weiner and Simpson 1989: 318). Thus, though originally restricted to specific words or phrases, the meaning has evolved to encompass adjectival usage applicable to describing any phenomena. As *The Oxford Companion to the English Language* notes 'The term is widely used to refer to any social, artistic, literary, dramatic, cinematic, or other formula that through overexposure has, in the view of a commentator, become trite and common place' (McArthur 1992: 222).

This use is also supported sociologically as can be seen in the way that Zijderveld (1979) also recognises that acts and even thoughts can be described as clichéd. Cliché functions to obviate the necessity of dealing with the full meaning of interaction utterances (ibid.: 10): clichés 'enable us to interact mechanically [...], without reflection. By means of clichés we are able to interact and communicate smoothly, routinely and in a facile manner' (ibid.: 58).

More contemporary analysis emphasises how clichés (Anderson-Gough et al. 1998) or similar discursive practices (Watson 2004) are implicated in the control of people in organisations. This view of the broader implications of cliché use is epitomised in what Davis has written of clichés in more generic fashion: a cliché 'stresses a saying's loss of vitality, which sedates rather than awakens its audience' (1999: 247). I do not deny this control or sedative function, but my ontological focus on the self-identity construction of the entrepreneur suggests that a more constructive emphasis is also appropriate: in other words cliché use both smoothes over to effect control and exert influence over the self and others, but also serves to smooth over the rugged and inconsistent terrain of individual experience into a consistent and secure narrative. My emphasis is on the positive functions clichés play in making complex communicative social interaction and the crafting of selves possible and successful.

These more positive functions can also be seen in the origins of the word itself. Cliché comes 'from the French root *clicher*, "to set together, to consolidate"'. Thus cliché originally 'referred to the practice of typesetters, who would keep recurring "set phrases" in a special compartment of their print-trays in order to save the time and labour' (Hughes 1988: 94, original emphasis). Similarly Shapin has suggested that common sense linguistic items such as proverbs and clichés serve a variety of purposes including 'aids to action […] where absolute certainty is neither available nor rationally to be expected' (2001: 740).

There seems to be then, two broad social functions to the use of clichés. First, there is the negative use whereby clichés are used to suppress, smooth over and simplify by sedation. Second, clichés function in a positive manner to facilitate and enable action in complex and uncertain interaction situations.[1] But how do these usages of clichés relate to Paul and John's crafting of an entrepreneurial identity?

In bringing together elements of biographical self-narrative, individuals differentiate and order their experience. Paul and John do this. They claim various things in their talk: to be like something, to like certain things above other things, and to reject, or distance themselves from, other things. The manner in which Paul and John use clichéd narrative is also a way of indicating something: in their entrepreneurial talk about personal qualities and attributes and attitudes to institutional others they indicate and emphasise what they are *not* by holding themselves apart or in opposition from the things they imagine they are separate from. In Kärreman and Alvesson's terms they exhibit a 'negative identity' (2001: 84), a sense of themselves defined by what they oppose. The purpose of this oppositional differentiation is to create a sense of knowing where things and others are supposed to be in their narratives. In turn this knowledge makes action and decision making easier: in both the positive and negative sense above. This is because 'focused and committed action calls for simplified and unreflective decision making, the denial of ambiguity and recognition of the drawbacks of a preferred route' (ibid.: 83). But there is something further about the context of Paul and John's work that suggests that clichéd narratives are useful in creating a coherent entrepreneurial self-identity narrative.

The store of specifically entrepreneurial stories available to Paul and John is inherently limited even in their wider community of practice. They do not know or commonly deal with many other entrepreneurs as entrepreneurs. Rather than drawing upon direct experience, their use of the entrepreneurial cliché sees them use public and cultural narratives (Somers 1994: 620): narratives that are, as it were, available off the shelf.

Hence, we can define the use of clichés as a widely available and adaptable public discourse and a resource which serves to consolidate self-narratives into a coherent sense of self-identity. The clichéd narrative that Paul and John use comprises of connected sets of statements, concepts, terms and expressions that constitute a way of talking about personal qualities, attributes and attitudes in a manner that closely equates to, and reflects, commonly held and commonplace understandings and meanings of the entrepreneur, thus framing the way the social actor understands and acts with respect to being an entrepreneur (adapted from Watson 1995: 816).

Before we see how Paul and John use this resource, a word of caution is required. A cliché is defined thus, identified and highlighted from the 'view of a commentator' (McArthur 1992: 222). The sophisticate's cliché may be a startling innovation for others. Unsurprisingly Paul and John did not seem especially aware of what I heard as clichéd entrepreneurial talk. And also unsurprisingly, I didn't ask them (or Mark and Will) about my observations. In other related work (Down 2002) I explore the epistemological, analytical and ethical problems this raises in more detail. Here I think it sufficient to show my hand in a more explicit manner than elsewhere in this book where the empirical analysis has arguably been more evidently objective (the 'Methodological Appendix' touches on these issues too).

FEATURES OF ENTREPRENEURIAL CLICHÉ

The focus below is on the various entrepreneurial themes and topics of Paul and John's talk. These themes and topics are being defined as elements of a public narrative that is characterised by cliché. Some of the things that Paul and John said also include some phrases that are more obviously clichéd expressions or figures of speech and these are both highlighted in bold. There are four sections. The first three look at typical entrepreneurial talk about personal qualities and attributes (risk and bravery, ambition and growth, autonomy and self-sufficiency), the last at attitudinal narratives towards institutional others (bureaucracies and corporations).

Risk and Bravery

There are an array of qualities, attributes, attitudes and motivations commonly ascribed to the entrepreneur. One of these is a positive attitude and willingness to taking risks. Paul and John both talked about the risks they had taken in forming Fenderco. One evening for instance, Paul and I were talking over a few beers in his living room before going to The Grinning Cat in time for last orders. The conversation turned to the topic of running businesses and being entrepreneurs. After I had said a few things about my own experiences of running a business, Paul described how

> there are very few people that I have worked with or for that are **prepared to take that risk to run their own business**. And that's what sets entrepreneurs above employees (most of them), for most. ... For many people their personal objective is the security of having a job and **not wanting to put anything on the line**.

Paul perceives the notion of taking risks as setting the entrepreneur 'above' or apart from employees in some way: the implication is that for Paul entrepreneurs choose to create their own security and do not have to rely on institutional others. Implicit is a rejection of, or a creation of distance from, those others. The quote also suggests that putting something 'on the line', of taking risks with being and feeling secure in life, is a positive personal attribute. The juxtaposition against 'employees' is also an indication that Paul sees himself as separate from employees and together with other entrepreneurs, because of his willingness to sacrifice security. But Paul is imagining this community of entrepreneurs (it is discursively and culturally assumed). By the use of this entrepreneurial cliché Paul de-emphasises or relegates other possible narratives.

Though relegated, these other narratives are nevertheless present in Paul's talk and can be seen in certain incongruent statements that lay threaded through the preponderance of entrepreneurially clichéd talk. For instance another time we were at the office chatting about Paul's school days and early work history, he started talking about his aborted attempt to start his own company with John whilst working for Harbourco

> ten years ago in our late twenties we were planning behind the scenes to form our own company, I think a lot of the ideas of today's company started then. [...] The problem ten years ago was **we were not brave enough.** We had a joint venture partner who was prepared to work with us [...]. We were in the right place and the right time; we just **didn't have the balls** to do anything. We didn't understand enough about life and business and the whole financial mechanisms of running companies. This is something we learnt after that period and as our careers developed with the new [merged corporate EuroPort] company, and they taught us how it works.

Paul says that to be successful in business one has to take risks and be brave. There is a contradiction here between Paul saying that if they had of been braver they may have started their firm earlier, and the realisation that they were not knowledgeable, learned or mature enough at that time anyway. The entrepreneurial cliché of being brave and willing to take risks is incongruent with these more rational considerations. Nevertheless, despite this recognition of rational considerations in the decision, the dominant idea in these two quotes is the importance of being willing to take the risk. Somehow, and notwithstanding the human ability to combine different rationalities (Brunsson 1985; Holliday 1995), the clichéd talk of risk provides a way of combining the non-entrepreneurial acts of not starting their firm earlier with a sense of himself now as an entrepreneur. The non-entrepreneurial past is explained by, and smoothly joined to the entrepreneurial present.

This is not to suggest that the risks that Paul and John have taken in 'stepping off into the abyss' (a phrase John used to describe their decision to start Fenderco) are not real in their effects. The threat of business failure and the related anxiety in the early months of Fenderco's existence were very real experiences. It is not just the talk that contributes to the formation and maintenance of a self-identity. Overcoming the challenge of events thrown up by engagement with social structures (supply of credit, market competition and so on) may be translated into meaning through talk and thought, but the engagement is real enough. As Giddens suggests, the seeking of thrills and the taking of risks is based on the expectation that they will be overcome: that a coherent narrative can be crafted. Self-identity is tested and 'mastery of such dangers is an act of self-vindication and a demonstration, to the self and others, that under difficult circumstances one can come through' (1991: 133).

The entrepreneurially clichéd talk of risk and bravery is not simply empty rhetoric or bluster. The cliché is far more useful and substantial than that, and supports the fluent expression of a coherent narrative. As Zijderveld has noted, clichés 'are not the "real" answers to precarious situations, but they do function, in particular they enable us to continue to communicate, as it were, on the safe surface' (1979: 62). The entrepreneurial clichéd narrative of risk and bravery provides a 'safe surface' with which Paul and John can deal with or not worry about the occasional precariousness of their entrepreneurial situation. The cliché (as a safe and consolidated interpretation of experience) provides, in Giddens' terms, coherence to the ongoing narrative of the self (1991: 54).

Ambition and Growth

Another prominent aspect of Paul and John's talk and an entrepreneurial commonplace is their expansive personal ambition and a desire to see their firm grow. During the time I visited Fenderco, the company was settled and prospering after a difficult start-up period. Paul and John were keen to expand the scope of the company and various new ventures were started. In addition to Steel Applications and CDL (Paul and John's 'moneybox' company which dealt with their personal pension investments and other financial dealings), which I mentioned in previous chapters, Paul talked vaguely about having set up a company to exploit his father's electronics expertise, and a design and consultancy company. (This desire for expansion was reflected in some of Paul's comments about how he felt that he had 'a bigger ambition for this company. We are going to grow'.) They were people on the move.

Steel Applications' activities initially centred on the building and installation of steel structures associated with Fenderco fendering systems. Steel Applications would tender and contract for steel structures related to the fender systems, such as supporting structures, ladders and guardrails. The steel would be purchased; a sub-contractor factory in the North of England would then manufacture, build and install the ladders, rails and so on. However, Paul's intentions for Steel Applications were more ambitious

> And this is all phase one, if you like, of this new company [Steel Applications]. We intend to go into production, and I am hopeful that this time next year … [pause]. We are seriously considering buying some land …[pause].
> *And building a factory?*
> Either building a factory or buying the existing factory.

And, about a year later when the contracted factory experienced some difficulties an opportunity arose to purchase it, and Fenderco took it over.

One of the underlying reasons, Paul said, for this desire for growth was the increasing 'boredom' in relation to core Fenderco activities. One evening in his living room Paul explained that

> I do find the work with Fenderco a little bit boring. That's why we've gone off, perhaps on a tangent, with this new company [Steel Applications]. I have been doing it [working with fendering systems] for a rather long time, you know. John and I have big egos, and I'd like us to be involved with more than just fenders. There is so much more that we could sell, and use our expertise to expand.

Paul's desire to grow and diversify Fenderco is deeply rooted. On one occasion, before the diversification into Steel Applications, and whilst driving to visit a project site, we were nearing the docks and happened to drive past a steel factory. Paul talked about visiting the docks and nearby beaches as a child and about how he had always been fascinated with the 'dead steam engines' that had lain derelict in the area then. Then, in one of the more colourful moments of the research Paul joked that seeing the steel works 'aroused' him and gave him a 'hard-on'. Paul explained

> I really want a factory one day.
> *Is that the 'toy' that you want?*
> I have got the products to put in it. I just need the production now.

In taking over Steel Applications he achieved this aim. Paul and John's ambition went further than this though. As Paul commented

> Both John and I were talking the other night considering possibilities for the future and – **we both have difficulties in working with other companies you know, and … [with] big firms** – but the one formula we know that works is John and I, working together. I mean, what if we sold out? You know, looked in the *Financial Times* and found another company. Turn it around, you know: **build up our own little empire**. Who knows!

This desire to 'build' a 'little empire', in Paul's imagination of a successful entrepreneurial future at least, was not necessarily dependent on the existence of Fenderco, or even continuing to work with fenders. Paul's boredom with fendering, the company diversification and his success as a business owner suggests that he felt that fenders were somehow beneath their ability and aspirations. Not only did Paul say he was a little bored, he also said immediately before the above quote, in answer to a question about how the company was faring, that he was

> Very happy. If somebody came along tomorrow with exactly the right …, you know, the money was right, then perhaps I'd sell it and go off and do something else.
> *Yeah, for what reason? Why, and what's the motivation in that: has it become mundane?*
> No, no, **it's just a new challenge.** [We are] **constantly trying to reinvent ourselves**.

In Paul's talk of his ambitions the possibilities of the future are not bounded by the company he has set up. He is identifying himself through the entrepreneurial cliché of ambition as someone who rejects and opposes the mundanity and boredom of running Fenderco or selling fenders. The narrative practice being employed is again an entrepreneurial cliché: routine is eschewed, freedom of choice is boundless; and business is but a vehicle for creativity and success, not something that one is attached too. These themes uncannily resemble the classic notion of the entrepreneur as destructive creator, one who toils against routine (Schumpeter [1934]1990).

And yet the desire to own a factory seems incongruous when set against the entrepreneurial cliché. Other talk about the commitment and effort he puts into his work and building up Fenderco seems similarly out of place.

One Saturday lunchtime at The Grinning Cat towards the end of the fieldwork Paul talked about an offer they had received from a Mediterranean-based competitor to buy Fenderco. Paul said that according to his sources in the industry the offer was in fact a poorly disguised attempt by his previous employers (EuroPort) to buy out Fenderco. Paul said that he 'didn't go through all that pain and risk [of setting up Fenderco] just to see myself back with the company that had treated me so badly'.

Once the factory had been purchased the responsibility for keeping it and its eighteen workers in work lay with Fenderco. Unfortunately orders for Fenderco fendering systems went through something of a minor slump towards the end of the research period and this meant that Steel Applications, which had also not generated as much external business as Paul had hoped, was losing money. One evening in the pub Paul expressed some doubts about the wisdom of buying the factory in the first place and also expressed some fears about keeping the men working.

The possibilities of selling Fenderco were also discussed more realistically too. At one point I tried to clarify what was happening in respect to the complex diversification and start-up of new companies and exactly why Paul felt he might sell Fenderco

You've got four/five companies, and they're all doing very well. So [when you say you might sell up] do you mean in terms of selling say, the core company, which is Fenderco, do you mean just that, I mean concentrating on something totally different, or do you mean shifting over to one of the other current firms?
I think we would at some stage probably sell Fenderco. Once ... [pause], and it's almost self sufficient at present, although we don't have anybody to replace John and myself [...]. [It would be difficult to] find somebody in the market somewhere who could fill our shoes. Fenderco would be good investment. [...]. There are companies that are interested in us. If we did sell, it would probably be linked to some sort of retainer fee, working directors or possibly smaller shareholders, who'd have a vested interest in continuing the economic growth of the company. But they may not be interested in the steel side of things or in more than one operation.
So in other words it's not necessarily selling up shop and living the life of Riley, it's about shifting into slightly different areas and putting more energy into that.
Yeah.

Again as with risk, the incongruent interplay between the mundane and engaged reality of managing Fenderco, and the clichéd talk of grand entrepreneurial futures seems not to threaten or disturb the coherence of Paul's main entrepreneurial narrative. Despite the rejection of stultification that the clichéd talk of growth and ambition provides it also accommodates the more mundane and occasionally anxiety-inducing reality of life in Fenderco. The hopes for the planned future and the constraints and limitations of the present are consolidated into clichéd and action-enabling coherence.

These statements about the future and the present reflect Giddens' conception of how 'under conditions of modernity' individuals draw the future into the present 'by means of the reflexive organisation of knowledge environments' (1991: 3). The future is colonised, but as that future can never be completely known, individuals will inevitably tend to engage in thinking about the risks of their projects (ibid.: 4). In Paul's case, the very real and unknowable risks (what Giddens calls 'imponderables') of business failure are partly overcome through use of entrepreneurially clichéd talk.

Zijderveld's discussion of clichés similarly argues that they represent part of the way we respond to 'unanswerable precarious situation[s]' (1979: 62). Specifically, Zijderveld argues that because clichés replace the need to engage fully with reflection and meaning, they bring a 'mechanical stability' (ibid.) to the difficult task of dealing with imponderables. The use of entrepreneurial clichés acts to consolidate and provide coherence to Paul's self-identity where situations of high risk and indeterminacy might suggest threat. This does not mean however that the obvious anxiety or recognition of the specific dangers that Paul and John might feel is occluded. Rather, it is that the idea or definition that Paul has of himself as entrepreneur is not unduly questioned or threatened by those dangers.

Autonomy and Self-sufficiency

Another aspect of the entrepreneurial cliché is linked to the ambition to build a 'little empire', and the idea that risk is something that 'sets entrepreneurs above employees'. Entrepreneurs are often perceived to pride themselves on their self-sufficiency and both their ability and desire to be autonomous: to build an empire, sovereign and apart from others. In this Paul and John are no exception.

John was talking about the early, financially difficult days of Fenderco

> Well, it was a nerve-racking time. We only had **each other to rely on**. There was nobody else to say 'you are doing a great job', there was **nobody to bail us out totally**, and we got ourselves into this thing and you know if it was going to work **it was down to us and nobody else**.

John then went on to talk about how he had, initially encouraged by his parents, always been self-sufficient, as a teenager and a university student

> **I have always liked to be self-sufficient, I do not like to be reliant on other people**, if you want to be self-sufficient you have got to: (a) you have got to have some money and; (b) you have got to have objectives or at least know what you are going to do. And, I suppose that again was just from an early age I just knew **I wanted to be independent of other people and I did not like being told what to do**, never have done, it doesn't go down well.

Similarly in a conversation with Paul about what he likes about running a business he said

> I certainly enjoy my job. I like the creative side and [large] projects, and I want to go on with the way we operate and the reasons why we have been successful. Yeah emm ... **I enjoy the *freedom* of running my own company**, and we can **apply our knowledge in a totally free way**, and em, create a product for the customer, *you know I do enjoy that* [his emphasis].

Paul then said, repeating his entrepreneurial desire for growth, that 'the whole process [of running a business] doesn't stop. [...] I expect someday in the not too distant future to sell the business. Maybe not entirely, or maybe entirely, and I'll move on to something else, using the capital to **generate something new**'. I then asked Paul what was motivating this process, was it the money or the development of his career

I haven't really thought about what I'd do with the money, but, er I do have sort of ambition plans and I enjoy the trappings and that, and I enjoy the successful elements. Not having to worry. I enjoy seeing the bank balance at the end of the week. [...] It's a combination of the desire to have money and also work that I enjoy, I like very much.

Thus the choice of work, the choice to change the institutional structure of the work and a more generalised autonomy from anxiety brought about by success and wealth, are all features of what Paul enjoys about his working environment. John's emphasis seems more negative as he stresses independence from others and self-reliance. But the talk of the ability of money to enhance choice is similar, as is the general sense of a need or desire to be apart from others. Both use the entrepreneurial cliché to reject authority and oppose constraints on their choice.

In reality the firm is far from being on its own. The bonds that bind them to their joint venture partners, banks and so forth, are relegated to the level of the taken-for-granted in this talk. If the reality of their being 'totally free', 'independent of other people' and apart can be doubted, the importance of the feeling or desire to be apart from others is nonetheless a crucial narrative device for maintaining their sense of themselves. An example of this can be seen by looking at the way in which the desires for expansion and diversification were not without detractors or involvement from other parties in the joint venture.

As I first discussed in Chapter 4, the creation of Steel Applications brought suspicion from Ausfend and FendercoEurope. Ausfend in particular feared that Fenderco would divert resources away from the joint activities of the venture and into Fenderco's own new ventures. Paul described how at the AGM in Australia he and John faced a reprimand. Paul said

They don't understand our aggression [...] you know. They don't like it.
So you got pissed off with them and they got pissed off with you?
We don't kowtow to them. Fuck that! You know!
So what happened then?
Well they raised this issue in the board meeting [about the amount of trade between Fenderco and Steel Applications]. [...]. The whole hour was devoted **to reading the riot act**.
And was this something you expected?
No, it should have been a celebration. [...] We should have been celebrating another spectacular result. I mean our results ... [pause]. We've probably turned over more than the Australian operation. We represent eighty per cent of the total sales. We are very, very big. The 'parent' company! That's a joke. They [Ausfend] don't have any.... I mean we're part owned by [FendercoEurope] and they [Ausfend] have a shareholding in [FendercoEurope]. [...]. These old men [in Ausfend] want to retire. They want to take their investments, their royalties. They want control over it [the joint venture], but they don't have that because of the entrepreneurial nature of the joint venture [meaning the nature of Fenderco and FendercoEurope]. [...]. There

has been a lot of trade between us [Fenderco and Steel Applications]. But we advised Jurgen [the Managing Director of FendercoEurope] of this right from the outset. His advice was not to say anything to the bosses.
The 'bosses' being the Australians?
The Australians, yeah.

My interjection in this part of the conversation reflects my surprise in hearing the term 'bosses'. Of course I understood that the joint venture implied certain obligations, but this was the first time I had heard anything but the entrepreneurial talk of independence and autonomy. The talk of 'freedom' and the autonomy implied in the talk of ambition and growth seems odd when set against the constraints and obligations inherent in the joint venture relationship, and the subordinate aspects of the relationship between the 'parent/boss' and Fenderco.

Paul explained later in the same conversation that they have very little to do with Ausfend at an operational level and contact them 'hardly ever, ... once a month'. Hence, it would be wrong to see Paul's entrepreneurial talk of self-sufficiency, autonomy, ambition and growth, as empty rhetoric: the relationship with Ausfend was largely one between independent organisations. Nevertheless this does not obscure the incongruity between the entrepreneurial talk and the reality of the inherent mutual obligations of the broader joint venture relationship.

In this talk John can be seen to reject and oppose those in authority who attempt to tell him what to do, and Paul rejects and opposes the outmoded thinking of the 'old men': these entrepreneurial clichéd narratives help to define who they are. Talk of self-sufficiency, autonomy, ambition and growth help Paul and John consolidate and maintain an entrepreneurial sense of identity. In the next section I explore *what* they are attempting to be autonomous of, but the question of *why* they want or need to have this feeling, and how clichéd narratives contribute to meeting the need is worth asking now.

One way of answering this question is to say that Paul and John are talking like this to avoid confronting the banal reality of their petit bourgeois lives. Scase and Goffee (1980) have also written about how many owner-managers talk-up the more mundane realities of their work. They suggest that for many owner-managers this rhetoric was simply to make them feel better about their sometimes financially precarious, difficult and anxiety-inducing work. Paul and John on the other hand *are* successful, and they *are* entrepreneurs: the talk is not simply a case of self-affirming rhetoric. The gap between the cliché of autonomy and self-sufficiency and the reality is not so great, though a gap exists. Rather than the clichéd talk serving to obliterate reality, it serves to consolidate the different elements of their self-identity through delineating what they reject and oppose.

So, why this need or desire for autonomy? Sennett's discussion of autonomy and freedom in *Authority* (1981) can help explain why Paul and John talk in the way they do about these topics. Sennet argues that autonomy is sought after because its possession is thought to confer freedom

> many people have come to believe that to be autonomous is to be free [...]. In the minds of ordinary people, to control the flow of influence brings not so much the pleasures of domination but a chance to get in control of oneself. *Autonomy builds a barrier against the world; once shielded, a person can live as he or she wants* (ibid.: 116, emphasis added).

Sennett suggests that autonomy in social matters describes a person who is 'self-possessed' (ibid.: 84) and has mastery of him or herself. With autonomy one becomes an individual and extraordinary, and avoids being ordinary: 'a state of being which is shapeless, unremarkable, bland – in a word, an amorphous condition of life' (ibid.: 92). This search for autonomy has its downside for the individual. The danger is one becomes 'isolated, restless, and unfulfilled: to look for freedom through autonomy creates a terrible anxiety' (ibid.: 118).

These descriptions of autonomy uncannily resemble descriptions of the classical entrepreneur. They also resemble the clichéd talk of Paul and John. They also explain the reason why autonomy is pursued: it is to achieve control of one's self-identity, and to feel secure in the world. Just as the talk of taking risks is a way of testing one's personal mastery, to pursue autonomy is to attempt to be more than just 'shapeless' and ordinary, and to reject and oppose that world in defining their self-identity. To achieve that degree of self-possession, a way of talking that confirms and supports the activities which single out the extraordinary, would be a vital narrative tool and resource. In Paul and John's case a clichéd way of talking provides 'shape' by consolidating an array of disparate activities and relegating those incongruent elements which might give rise to feelings of being 'ordinary' and 'shapeless'.

However, in building a 'little empire', to reiterate Paul's ambition; or to create a 'barrier against the world', to be 'independent of other people' as John desired; to avoid being 'ordinary' or ensuring that you are above being an employee, as Paul put it; also paradoxically 'creates a terrible anxiety' (ibid.). Why? Because an individual who seeks to shut the world out also becomes a 'prisoner in the world [...] endlessly looking inside for a sense of fulfilment, as though the self were like a vast warehouse of gratification that one's social relations had kept one from exploring' (ibid.: 117–18; Taylor 1991: 35, makes a similar argument). In other words Sennett's argument is that one cannot be truly secure and free from anxiety or truly an individual unless one engages with others. This is something that the clichéd talk of Paul and John tends to deny. Something too, as we have seen in Chapter 3, that complements the way they attempt to over-control their relationships.

By using Sennett's explanation of autonomy in social life we can see that its possession is something like a poisoned chalice. The very pursuit of security and a refuge from anxiety produces the potential for its negation. But where is the anxiety in Paul and John's talk? Obviously the pursuit of security is a result of the attempt to overcome generalised existential anxiety (Giddens 1991), and the creation of Fenderco, I am suggesting, is a project ultimately attributable to this pursuit. Existential anxiety itself is arguably beyond the reach of the type of research employed here, and certainly in my many conversations with Paul and John there is little talk of personal angst, fallibility or fragility. And this is hardly surprising. However, my description of how the entrepreneurial cliché functions as a device to smooth out the discontinuities and consolidate narratives into a coherent and effective entrepreneurial identity, shows, at least, why anxiety for those like Paul and John can be mastered.

I have explained why autonomy is desired or needed by Paul and John and how the clichéd narrative they use contributes to its achievement. What I have not yet discussed beyond a sense of an abstract generalised other, is exactly what they are seeking to be autonomous from: what they are rejecting and opposing. In the following section I shift from a concern with personal qualities and attributes of the entrepreneur, to a more externally oriented focus on attitudes to institutional others: just what are Paul and John trying to avoid?

Bureaucracies and Corporations

Perhaps the most clichéd entrepreneurial cliché can be seen in John's talk about his attitudes to others, especially the authority embodied in bureaucracies and corporations. Paul is less vociferous, but shares similar attitudes towards large corporations. He said the following in relation to his father's influence on his entrepreneurialism

> I was influenced by my Father, I loved him, I worshipped him, I guess I went through school thinking, well I am not going to work for a big organisation and get stitched up by a load of ... [pause]. **I am going to do it for myself. It seemed to be the natural way to do it.**

John's clichéd ire against large bureaucratic corporations has a long history. As he tells it now, even whilst he was studying engineering at Imperial College London, John was set against taking up a graduate traineeship

> I didn't want to go and work for a corporation. I had loads of friends that went to work for companies like Rolls Royce and Ford and so on, and I have to say I wasn't

into those sort of graduate development schemes and all the rest of it.
You weren't into that?
Well, you know. They are now in **middle management jobs, quite cosy. They
have got their two point two kids and various dull lifestyles** and as a result I
don't really keep in touch with most of them, it is not the sort of thing I ever saw
myself doing.

John's own life differs from corporate middle management to the extent that
he runs his own firm. He has two children and his life might also be described
as 'cosy' in that he is well off and lives in a solidly middle-class house and
area. Many of his neighbours work for corporations. What John says that sets
him apart is his choice of an entrepreneurial career, the rejection of what he
sees as the secure, 'cosy' corporate career, and the inclusion of entrepreneurial
risk. The point here is that in his rejection of corporate sponsored suburban
dullness the differences with his ex-college friends are not so great in terms of
the actual lifestyle and the type of activities he pursues: John might drive a
TVR and not a Volvo, but the differences are essentially limited. What *is*
different is his sense of himself, a point to which I return below.

John continued with this theme at many points in our conversation, and at
one point he talked about how many of his student peers had done sandwich
courses, sponsored by large companies

In some ways I regretted [not having been sponsored] and in other ways I didn't.
They worked: they were always guaranteed a summer job and you know,
professional training, and they could go and get their [engineering] charter with
their employer, but then they were **locked** into being engineers. **It is very hard to
get out of that cycle [once] you are in.** It is like being an apprentice, you are in
there and **if you want to change … . You have been brainwashed into whatever
big company you are working for**, Ford, ICI or whatever. They all had their ways
of … what they wanted out of their employees, so they were making a long-term
investment, so **they had to get you thinking in the company way**. You could see
that in some of the guys I was working at college with.

A variety of the themes from the previous sections re-emerge in the above
talk: the sense in which John feels himself to be apart and more self-reliant
than the corporately dependent others, and the willingness to sacrifice and risk
the secure and 'cosy' life: the desire for autonomy. What is different in this
talk is the identification of membership with large organisations as the
antithesis of how he views himself. For John his denigrating rejection of large
organisations was a persistent and pervasive theme. For example, he talked
about his early career experience in a rubber and tyre corporation

I worked for [name of corporation] and **it was slow and plodding and nothing
happened quickly and it was tedious**, you know. If you wanted to get anything
done, anything made, whatever, it took weeks and weeks to get it through the

factory, you had loads of obstacles put in your way all the time. **If you wanted to circumvent the system you could never get round it or you could but it was so difficult and you really had to work hard to achieve things for the customers**.

And in comparison, when working in an entrepreneurial business making and selling kitchen stoves soon after graduating from university

we could achieve things, we could do things, **as a small group with three people we could achieve things. We made a decision and 'boom!' it would happen**: 'We are going to change'; I don't know, 'we are going to add this to our product range'; 'we are going to do a promotion on that' you know; or 'we are going to build something and make our own literature', you know. We would decide to do, and a week later it is done, you know. **You work for a big company, you decide to do it and once you have been through all the committee stages … . It is a bit like government. You know; a year later and everybody has lost interest in it and it fizzles out.**
So it is the immediacy that you like?
Yes, I suppose **an impatience to achieve things.**

This can also be seen in the way John talked about working at EuroPort. He talked of how he had felt increasingly detached from what he was doing.

I had built up lots and lots of orders by proxy through guys working for me […], but I lost touch with a lot of the regular customers. And I was getting a lot of flack from [the new corporate parent] and I was finding it frustrating because there was **too much paper work**, a lot of travel: **I was a company man, moved out of my main field and into this management thing.** [Paul and I were] **being told all the time […] that we must do things this way, that way**. We were getting very fed up […]. You couldn't spend tuppence on your expenses **without reporting to the head office**. It was pathetic really.

John also perceived the large corporation as a place where hard work and entrepreneurs did not fit easily. For instance he talked about one of his managers in the large rubber and tyre corporation he had worked for prior to starting with Harbourco

[Manager's name] was very much an entrepreneurial guy, he was a bit unorthodox in many ways, **he wasn't a natural fit in [the corporation]** so I suppose **I was never a natural fit**, although I worked quite well with him. **It was never hard work there, it was very lazy. People would vanish at four o'clock on Fridays and five o'clock on Mondays to Thursdays.**
Did that bother you?
Yes it did, I suppose. I actually felt quite bored because **the level of work was not intensive**.

Taken overall the subject of how things operate in larger organisations provides a negative arena for determining what John feels he is not. The clichés in these quotes are the antithesis to the entrepreneurially positive attributes and personal qualities. Rather than autonomy there is a lack of freedom of thought; working for a corporation means that one becomes 'brainwashed' and lack control. Rather than focusing immediately and directly on the needs of customers, the larger organisation gets in the way and creates obstacles to action. Rather than hard work, the large organisation encourages the easy life. Rather than unorthodox individualism being encouraged, it was seen as unnatural.

The previous discussion of obligations to the Ausfend 'bosses' and the similarities between John's lifestyle and the corporate manager suggest that there is some clash between this clichéd oppositional talk and reality, as in the other sections. John and Paul's work *is* different from work in a corporation. But regardless of the extent to which Paul and John's reality differs, the nevertheless cartoon-like characterisation of the anti-entrepreneurial corporation creates a straw man with which John (and to a lesser extent, Paul) can consolidate and competently narrate a sense of himself as entrepreneur. Incongruous events and thoughts that might show complex interdependencies and similarities between the two worlds can be safely relegated to an innocuous status, which will not unduly challenge his self-identity. The cliché makes sense and smoothes out the complex wrinkles of real life. In Zijderveld's (1979) terms the functionality of the cliché has superseded meaning and reflection.

CONCLUSION

The point of cliché as a characterising concept with which to encompass the narratives of enterprise that Paul and John use is to highlight the particularly public nature of their talk. There are many narrative aspects of entrepreneurial self-identity they use as resources. I have chosen cliché because it seemed interesting and central to their context as entrepreneurial small business owner-managers. The examples above and throughout this book also show that other narratives and specific discursive practices populate their self-identity talk too. I hope too that in carving up the water of narrative the way this and the other chapters have, it is nevertheless realised that conceptual characterisations are necessarily imprecise.

It should be clear for instance that some of what Paul and John say about being entrepreneurial may not be as clichéd as some other things they say. Attempting to work out the degree of authenticity, or the degree to which a given statement is part of a public or an ontological (experiential) narrative, is probably not feasible. As I have hopefully stressed, the argument in this chapter is that cliché *characterises* their talk about being entrepreneurs. What

Paul and John told me about these matters is not some easily identifiable and separate component of their narrative. I have created these separations; these book chapters.

What the characterisation does however is show how Paul and John mix and match public and ontological narratives to achieve a sense of themselves as entrepreneurs. Well-known narratives of enterprise are smoothly juxtaposed with more particular and often contradictory self-narratives. The Ausfend 'bosses' example, where the autonomy of Fenderco is shown as less than complete, demonstrates what happens when the dominant self-identity narrative of the entrepreneurial cliché is challenged. Resolving the challenge was partly achieved through reference to the dominant narrative (the 'old men' not understanding the entrepreneurial nature of the venture). But it was also consolidated and smoothed into an effective narrative by reference to a generational identity resource: the denigration of the 'old men' (see also Parker 2000; and Down and Reveley 2004).

The above empirical analysis consistently refers to Paul and John defining who they are by what they are not. Their being entrepreneurs is based on oppositional rather than propositional talk. They associate with the clichéd talk of entrepreneurialism as a way of articulating their opposition to certain ideas, types of people and institutions. The generalised object of this opposition is a confused and paradoxical pot-pourri of clichéd articulations against certain central concepts of modernity: there is talk of opposition to the shapeless and ordinary, suburban values, boredom, routine, authority, security, bureaucratic values and so on. Yet the incongruities and contradictions of their talk and actions in running Fenderco show that they also share some of the 'cosy' petit bourgeois and modern values they oppose. The oppositional narrative of the entrepreneurial clichés reconciles and puts a safe surface over these incongruities and contradictions.

Underlying their use of the off-the-shelf entrepreneurial clichéd narrative however is a deeper and dynamic process of self-identity crafting based on a search for autonomy (Sennett 1981: 116–18) and their journey away from being shapeless and ordinary: away from mundanity. Their adherence to the self-identity narratives of being entrepreneurs is therefore not necessarily fixed. It is a narrative strategy for producing a secure self-identity within the context of their current situation. Things change. Narratives and selves are recrafted. Creating a self reflects both fragile *and* robust feelings of self-identity.

> Fragile, because the biography the individual reflexively holds in mind is only one 'story' among many other potential stories that could be told about her development as a self; robust, because a sense of self-identity is often securely enough held to weather major tensions or transitions in the social environments within which the person moves. [Giddens 1991: 55]

I have shown how clichés are a tool which helps combine the fragile and robust aspects of personal identity in the occasionally stormy and infinitely populous seas of narrative and discourse. Our next and concluding chapter seeks to bring together the fragile and robust collation of concepts and experiences of this book as a whole into coherence. As we will see self-narratives do change, tools are themselves refashioned, jettisoned or reapplied.

NOTES

1. This divergence also reflects differing views on the use of clichés in spoken and written language: see for instance Bagnall's defense of cliché (1985) in contrast to the more orthodox and condemnatory Partridge ([1940]1979).

7. Conclusion

You get them wrong before you meet them, while you're anticipating meeting them;
you get them wrong while you're with them; and then you go home to tell somebody
else about the meeting and you get them all wrong again. Since the same generally
goes for them with you, the whole thing is really a dazzling illusion empty of all
perception, an astonishing farce of misperception. And yet what are we to do about
this terrible significant business of other people, which gets bled of the significance
we think it has and takes on instead a significance that is ludicrous, so ill-equipped
are we all to envision one another's interior workings and invisible aims? Is
everyone to go off and lock the door and sit secluded like the lonely writers do, in a
soundproof cell, summoning people out of words and then proposing that these words
are closer to the real thing than the real people that we mangle with our ignorance
every day? The fact remains that getting people right is not what living is about
anyway. It's getting them wrong that is living, getting them wrong and wrong and
wrong and then, on careful reconsideration, getting them wrong again. That's how
we know we're alive: we're wrong. Maybe the best thing would be to forget being
right or wrong about people and just go along for the ride. But if you can do that –
well, lucky you.
Philip Roth *American Pastoral* (1998: 35)

AN EPILOGUE OF SORTS

All things come to an end. It was November 1998 when I stopped researching Fenderco. During the research a major change to the lives of Paul and John did not occur. The story of Fenderco I have told so far is therefore very much one of business as usual. But their narratives about the past can be read like the hastily assembled histories of tenuous and aspirational nations. Though the historical records of their talk say much about how they perceive and talk of themselves now, they can only give vague hints and clues to how they might have once perceived and spoke of themselves. The stories they tell serve immediate and short-term purposes.

And these stories and the lives at Fenderco continued in this vein. I made occasional social visits to Maltonbury up until I emigrated in March 2000, starting a new life in Australia. When I visited Maltonbury in July 2001 it seemed as though Fenderco had been turned upside down. Paul and John were no longer owner-managers or entrepreneurs. Paul was no longer living in the 'castle house' or Maltonbury. Both were now separated from their wives. Things were very different in many ways, and these changes though not part of the formal research are instructive, and provide a good starting point with which to conclude.

I had arranged to meet Paul at the office. Immediately on walking into the now fully renovated offices, I knew the changes I had heard about from Paul and others had transformed the character of Fenderco. Mark had moved on and was working elsewhere. There were three new employees. Despite the reduction in work space the office was less cluttered. Whilst I waited for Paul, I wandered through and spoke to the others. It was good to see John and Will again, but the previous easy familiarity was missing. We didn't dither in our conversations. The whole place seemed more professional and anonymous than it had been. I had become a stranger again.

With Paul things were more familiar and we left for a lengthy lunch in a local pub. Not The Grinning Cat; he didn't go there now. We discussed the progress of my new life down under, the Fenderco research, what had happened to Paul and John and their company, his marriage and many other things besides. I was shocked at how much had changed. In amongst the everyday conversation I wondered if Paul would still present himself as an entrepreneur.

Paul explained how John and he were no longer joint managing directors of Fenderco UK. Nor did they run the other subsidiary firms. Paul said that either these had never really got started, had been subsumed within Fenderco UK, or had ceased trading. Anyhow involvement in these ventures had ceased. They were no longer entrepreneurs. They had both become employees of a new company formed from the merger of Fenderco UK, FendercoEurope and a new European corporate parent (the 'old men' of Ausfend were not now involved). This new parent company was the same corporation (EuroPort) which had originally bought out Harbourco: the same corporation that Paul and John had in part formed Fenderco to be rid of; the same corporation that had treated Paul so poorly when working for them in Asia.

Paul was well aware of the circular irony of this. In essence he had his old job back, but at a much higher level. The senior personnel of the old EuroPort had moved on or retired. It was different company now with different attitudes. Paul and John could work with them now.

Why the change? The major rationale, aside from the realisation of capital that Paul and John benefited from, was to rationalise operations and to avoid market coverage and functional duplication between Fenderco UK and FendercoEurope. Paul took on responsibilities for design engineering and project management and John worked on sales and marketing. According to Paul this restructuring had had a profound effect on his relationship to John and to work generally. 'Friday night' at The Grinning Cat is no longer a Fenderco institution. Paul said that he would not now be a close friend with John if it weren't for work. They don't spend so much time together socially now they are not running the company.

These fragments of fact and conversational filaments compare poorly to the lush complexity of previous chapters, but their significance is clear. Given the extent to which Paul and John identified so strongly with the role of the entrepreneur and narratives of enterprise I asked Paul how he felt about his not now being an entrepreneur: he didn't really miss running his own company. He is now doing what he's best at – design engineering. That's who he is now.

Was Paul's entrepreneurial self purely bluster? Had he been hiding a different person underneath the talk? Had he been lying about the importance of his relationship with John? The answer to these questions has to be no. The degree of fabrication needed to create and sustain these false impressions is simply not credible. Despite the previous importance of entrepreneurialism to his story, the way in which self-identity works allows for no hidden or inner self beyond the 'depth-psychological' (Kärreman and Alvesson 2001: 63) and genetic dispositions. Instead there is an elastic, contextually contingent and actively constructed collation and maintenance of self-identity narratives. Stories are invented, shaped and emphasised depending on circumstances and events.

Paul's adherence to an entrepreneurial narrative would not now be appropriate. As Sennett has it 'a person's life-narrative [...] has to be continually recast in the course of experience; you need continually to make a fresh explanation of yourself' (2000: 177). The circumstances of Paul's life in relation to his entrepreneurial talk (Chapter 6), of personal and financial risk, attitudes to corporations, ambition and growth, and autonomy and self-sufficiency, have shifted. Paul's use of the Fenderco locale (the 'castle house', the pub, the office) which reflected the all-encompassing nature of his entrepreneurial self-identity is less expansive than it was (Chapter 5). The Fenderco office is a more separate, distant and professional place now. The manner in which generational narratives are used to emphasise an 'entrepreneurial' break with the past (Chapter 4), might now become relegated to more general acknowledgement of generational difference. The changes also suggest that the dyadic isolation and mutual codependence of his relationship with John (Chapter 3), and the co-option of employees, is not now needed.

I have little idea which of these narratives has been retained, how they may have been reconfigured to account for Paul's new life, or what has been invented and promoted to replace talk not now appropriate. But no doubt many of the stories Paul tells may still include talk of generations, autonomy and so forth. However Paul tells it, they are not likely to be used to emphasise an entrepreneurial self-identity. Why would he, when he is not an entrepreneur?

In understanding the seeming elasticity of their entrepreneurial narrative it is worth reiterating that in the previous chapter I characterised their narratives as publicly available resources. The stories they used were off-the-shelf, not their own. In this sense their entrepreneurial narratives might be described as weak or superficial. Sennett has written about what makes for 'strong' and 'weak' identities, and has suggested that the 'capacity to recast your life-story is a sign of strength in attending to the world outside. Correspondingly, a weak identity means clinging to a rigid image of self, a lack of capacity to revise when circumstances require it' (2000: 177). Even from these post-research fragments Paul *is* clearly able to recast his narratives. Bespoke or ready-made, the strength of a self-identity narrative is the ability to recast the story.

Sennett also argues that those individuals who can deal with the ambiguity of identity and include the disjunctive and conflicting elements of their life narrative, have a dense identity and are attracted to situations where the 'edges' of the different narratives meet: 'the "edge" is a zone of engagement' (ibid.: 178); 'a young lawyer who feels affection and solidarity for elders he does not professionally respect' has 'density of self' (ibid.). Paul and John also expressed similar ambiguities in their generational narratives when talking about their previous employers at Harbourco. In these terms some of Paul and John's narratives show a willingness to deal with the ambiguous edges of their self-identities.

On balance though their story is about creating buffers and controlling rather than engaging with the edge. In Sennett's sense their identities were 'weak'. The need to focus on the entrepreneurial problems at hand meant that 'simplified and unreflective decision making' and 'the denial of ambiguity and recognition of the drawbacks of a preferred route' were useful strategies to follow (Kärreman and Alvesson 2001: 83). Now that the entrepreneurial contexts (including the very real risks and responsibilities of running a firm) for establishing this protected and 'weak' identity have evaporated, Paul and John are perhaps likely to craft and emphasise other self-narratives. Paul might emphasise or promote design engineering, aesthetic and creative narratives. John might promote sales and 'fun' narratives (he would often talk about work being or not being 'fun'). In Sennett's sense they may be developing 'stronger' self-identities as a result. How these changes in their self-identities will manifest themselves is for the future. Even without the above epilogue this book has shown that self-identity as narratively conceived is a transient, elastic and dynamic process.

Despite all this Paul and John's narratives do have consistency and are consolidated. The changes in the context of Paul and John's lives have not transformed them into unrecognisably different people. A journey is travelled and their narratives incorporate the flux and disjunction of life. We all bring baggage (those residues of previous entanglements) into our new relationships. We all have stories that need to be used but don't fit our current selves. It all helps provide material with which to draw on when the circumstances of life change.

THE REAL THING

It's probably not a good idea to make false starts when trying to bring something to a close. It should be clear that we nevertheless needed to know of these changes to Paul and John's lives. They change the nature of my conclusions.

So what do *I* think the reader should take from this book? First we should reiterate the main points of the empirical chapters.

Chapter 3, 'Relationships', showed that Paul and John's relational narratives provide an emotional refuge which enables them to be effective entrepreneurs; and to realise and create an entrepreneurial sense of self. This is achieved by creating a substitute intimacy in their relationships at work. Their insular search for authenticity prompts excessively monological narratives. As a result they become the willing victims of a self-centred and 'narcissistic' mode of contemporary culture (Taylor 1991: 35). Like many they suffer from 'the illusion of atomistic self-sufficiency' (Rose 1996: 156).

The concern of Chapter 4, 'Generations', was how Paul and John used their narrative of generational encounters as an important self-identity resource in thinking of themselves as entrepreneurs. They used generational narratives both to explain the beginning of their entrepreneurial careers and as a continuing narrative resource differentiating themselves as 'young gun' entrepreneurs. Generational narrative resources provided for a purposeful sense of a dislocation from the past way of doing things. Again Paul and John's narratives set them in opposition to others: individual and isolated. Again their narratives attempt to deny the inevitable dialogic essence of the social relations that create the self.

Chapter 5, 'Space', showed that crafting an entrepreneurial identity has a spatial characteristic: Paul and John craft their narratives and present themselves to suit the various locations they inhabit. We saw that they attempt to control the different locations they inhabit, to varying degrees of success. Their attempts to individualise their sense of place in the world can only partially succeed because they again cannot control or avoid dialogic engagement with others in all of these spaces. Paul and John cannot shut out the world or remake it in their own image.

In Chapter 6, 'Clichés', I showed how Paul and John mixed and matched the public and ontological narratives of enterprise in a clichéd way to help support their sense of themselves. Narratives of enterprise are used predominately to define who they are in a negative sense: they define themselves as entrepreneurs by what they oppose. This way of talking acts to smooth away the incongruities and contradictions thrown up by events and experiences – past and present – that don't fit the dominant entrepreneurial story. Underlying the clichéd entrepreneurial narrative itself is a deeper and dynamic process of self-identity crafting based on a search for autonomy (Sennett 1981: 116–18) and authenticity; their journey away from being shapeless and ordinary. Again their narratives seek to individualise their world.

These simple summaries of the empirical chapters suggest a strong link between the different narratives; that they form a coherent whole; that the story – my story – does hang together. That's okay, but we need to explore this a little more. What we need to do now is to assess the broader relevance of these findings. There are two aspects to this. First, I comment on Paul and John's narrative crafting in relation to contemporary debates about modernity and the place of the individual, and in particular, the enterprising individual. Second, the place of Paul and John as enterprising individuals is discussed in the light of recent discussions of the role of enterprise in society. In both these sections I suggest some ways in which enterprise and organisational scholars may need to take account of this book.

Home Alone

How do Paul and John's strategies for forming an entrepreneurial self compare to broader notions of self-identity? Why are they trying to isolate themselves; to create a hideout? Does the manner in which they use their resources represent a counter-reaction to modernity? Or, is theirs just an attempt like everyone else, to create a sensible story, one that works?

Each empirical chapter has provided resources with which to answer these questions. In Chapter 3 I argued that their talk of friendship was in part an affective or emotional refuge from some of the impersonal forces of modernity. Generational narratives in Chapter 4 were part of a traditional language of renewal, co-opted and translated for modernity. Similarly, in Chapter 5 I wrote that Paul and John's attempt to control much of the Fenderco locale might be seen as a part of the way that 'individuals attempt to reconstruct traditional locality and spatial embeddedness in reflexive projects of the self' (Giddens 1991: 206–7).

Chapter 6 did not explicitly address this issue, but the use of clichés also represents and reflects differences between past and present, tradition and modernity. Clichés are linked to mimetic pre-modern narratives of repetition and emulation: 'in clichés pre-modern consciousness has been preserved and carried over to modernity', 'they seem to constitute survivals of magical techniques by which human beings, throughout the ages, have satisfied some deep-seated needs for security, stability and certainty' (Zijderveld 1979: 62, 65). If correct, Paul and John are perhaps using their clichéd narrative as a way of narratively reconstructing or re-imagining their own self-identities in the image of the more certain identities of traditional and pre-modern times (Giddens 1991: 206–7).

Written in summary form it seems like Paul and John are building their castles to some master plan in a very traditional style. Paul and John *are* in part engaged in the various 'counter-reactions' and reconstructions of tradition within the context of the disembedding of time and space typical of high modernity (ibid.: 147, 206). But Paul and John are *re*constructing tradition and forming something new in the process. They are not fighting a rear-guard action to hold onto a tradition that is slipping away in the face of modernity. Giddens' analysis also recognises how a person's attempt to reconstruct traditional relationships to time, space and the 'lifespan' serves to create new and modern self-identities rather than simply an impossible reclamation of the past. He writes

> The disembedding mechanisms [of high modernity] intrude into the heart of self-identity; but they do not 'empty out' the self any more than they simply remove prior supports on which self-identity was based [that is tradition]. Rather, they allow the self (in principle) to achieve much greater mastery over the social relations and social contexts reflexively incorporated into the forging of self-identity than was previously possible. [ibid.: 148–9]

Paul and John are engaged in a project of the self as well as running Fenderco. The 'in principle' in the above quote presumably refers to the variable opportunity and capacity (that is power, money and so on, depending on the particular context) that individuals will have to achieve this 'mastery'. In Paul and John's case the narrow institutional contexts of Fenderco allows them a good deal of mastery. However, the over-protective cocoon they have created is also a particularly limited and claustrophobic domain. Paul and John reconstruct tradition to the extent they do to provide them with the 'fixity' necessary for taking the risk inherent in their venture.

But one might more practically ask, aren't Paul and John just simply trying to make some money, trying to find – as we all are – something they think is meaningful to do with their lives? Isn't all my speculation about how they embody and juxtapose traditional and modern narratives simply looking for unnecessarily hidden meaning and motives? Isn't it all just sociologese?

Outside of the current conceptual context I think this is fair comment. However, it is worth reiterating the purpose of this book. It is concerned with providing a description of self-identity processes related to acting entrepreneurially, and adding to, and clarifying the vocabulary that is used in that description. This book has responded to the challenge Somers set, that social science needs to 'devise a vocabulary that we can use to reconstruct and plot over time and space the ontological narratives and relationships of [...] actors, the public and cultural narratives that inform their lives, and the crucial intersection of these narratives with the other relevant social forces' (1994: 620).

I am intent on explicating the social meaning of these processes, not in some way improving how self-identity or life is done. Yes, Paul and John are simply doing what we all do in telling their lives, and this book has not uncovered hidden meaning in what they do as such. Mine is not the only description. To succeed as a new vocabulary, to resonate and to be useful, the description offered here needs to meet 'some particular need which a given community happens to have at a given time' (Rorty 1989: 37). I can't determine this need. But new descriptions, new vocabularies have an affect. The entrepreneur as economic rational man; as a bundle of traits and as Schumpeterian superhero have all met these needs. But new realities create new needs and we need a way of seeing *how* narrative practices of entrepreneurial self-identity are created. Key to this *how* has been the strongest and most obvious central theme of Paul and John's narratives. I refer to the individualistic and oppositional manner in which this traditional enclave or over-protective cocoon is achieved through their narratives.

All the empirical chapters show that Paul and John identify themselves as entrepreneurs in an oppositional manner. This oppositionalism is twinned with an individualistic and atomistic view of the world. Both Sennett (1981: 117–18) and Taylor (1991: 35) argue that this solipsistic feature of self-identity in modernity is a denial of the inherently dialogic and interactive process of achieving self-identity (see also MacIntyre 1981: 240; and Rorty 1989: 41).

I have shown that Paul and John cannot really achieve their solipsistic aim: they cannot oppose and cut themselves off from everything. Taylor too, despite his disquiet at how people pursue self-identity in cultures of authenticity, implies that because identity is 'inherently' dialogic then attempts to create it monologically must ultimately fail. Taylor further argues that an attempt to create an 'inwardly generated identity' means that individuals also become vulnerable to a need for recognition (1991: 49). If an individual has an overarching need for individual authenticity and originality, then this needs to be recognised by others to be meaningful. Modern self-identity is a process of 'self-discovery' and that 'revelation comes through expression' (ibid.: 61). For Paul and John their project of Fenderco is an expression of their originality and authenticity for which they hope for and receive recognition. This recognition, as was shown in Chapter 3, is supplied by each other and the co-opted attentions of Mark and Will.

Implicit in Taylor, Rorty, Sennett and Giddens' arguments is a moral stance. As I have been writing and thinking about Paul and John, as you have been reading about them, we have been making judgements and evaluating their behaviour and words from the point of view of our own 'evaluative criteria' (Somers 1994: 617). I have tried to avoid being judgemental about what Paul and John say and do. Paul and John have their failings like every one of us.

Moral judgements are not simply a matter of personal opinion. Value is inherently secreted in human activity: any action or narrative will impact upon others in different ways, affecting the intentions, purposes, reasons and beliefs of agents (MacIntyre 1981: 80).

So what is my position?

Paul and John's narratives do tend to reflect some of the atomistic and narcissistic coping strategies of modern life. Indeed 'self-referentiality of manner is unavoidable in our culture' (Taylor 1991: 82). However, Taylor makes a distinction which shows that despite our inability to avoid the atomistic culture in creating our self-identities, there may be some means of redemption.

Taylor distinguishes between the 'manner' and the 'matter' or 'content' of action and concludes that individuals will only find genuine fulfilment in action 'which has significance independent of us or our desires' (Taylor 1991: 82). Though Paul and John might not be able to avoid self-referentiality in the way they talk about themselves and their actions, what they actually do and produce is of consequence. Taylor's argument suggests that it is in Paul and John's material and social achievements through Fenderco (the jobs they create and the fenders they build, and not the glass castles of their personal desire) that they can find 'genuine fulfilment' in creating their self-identity. And we have seen that in addition to the narratives of enterprise, other narratives which reflect those things that 'stand beyond' Paul and John's self-referential 'desires and aspirations' (Taylor 1991: 82) are also present. Narratives of aestheticism and a regard for beauty, pride in work done well, providing a good service to the customer, design excellence and a satisfaction in solving problems, a desire to produce things, and so on, are all there together with the entrepreneurial.

And, as the above account of my later conversation with Paul suggests, the self-referentiality of his entrepreneurialism has now abated. Both Paul and John are perhaps now more connected with these other narratives, and are consequently identifying themselves with the 'wider whole' of modern society (ibid.: 91). This is probably a good thing for them and those that work with them.

This analysis perhaps reflects broader doubts about the moral implications of the enterprise society (du Gay 2000b) where 'bimoral' conflicts between market and traditional moralities (Hendry 2004) emerge as the central problem in managing organisations. Paul and John's engagement with enterprise discourse provides a good example of how individuals use and reconstruct discourses of enterprise to create coherent selves, in the face of conflicting moralities.

Narratives of Enterprise

We have seen that there are some personal costs to using entrepreneurial narratives in the way that Paul and John did. Given the extent to which narratives of enterprise are currently seen and heard in society, maybe many others pay a similar price in constructing entrepreneurial self-narratives. Questioning entrepreneurialism in this way seems to me quite a daring thing to say (though as mentioned above there are others doing the same), such is the ubiquity of positive interpretations. Governments, corporations, churches and universities all clamour to sing the praises of the enterprising spirit. My own university has 'entrepreneurs in residence' and 'visiting professors', that have previously run successful entrepreneurial ventures. Students run their own businesses as part of their degrees. Television shows are making minor celebrities of minor entrepreneurs. It seems that everyone wants to be his or her own boss: which is just as well. Behaving enterprisingly is seen as a contemporary economic necessity in an era of efficient labour markets where people need to provide initiatives for their own employment. Shifting population demographics mean that state-led welfare will not provide as wide a safety net as it once did. Corporations look for enterprise in their managers: etcetera, etcetera. There is a long list of reasons why enterprise represents a contemporary prominent discourse. Whatever the politics, debates, or explanations, enterprising self-responsibility is clearly a mantra of our times.

The tale I tell in this book is something of a palliative to this feast. The lack of thinking that often goes with positive renditions of enterprise is worrying given the degree to which our institutions are restructuring themselves based on such a vague and catch-all notion. I do not however hold with those nay-sayers at the opposite end that denigrate the achievements of the enterprising. Those that seek to represent enterprise as the driving metaphor of civil and moral collapse are as guilty as those that promote it as an epoch defining curative. Paul and John's story shows that behaving entrepreneurially is a contingent and elastic narrative strategy: a strategy both mundane and pragmatic, and not without its drawbacks.

In truth this story has not been about 'The Entrepreneur', that mythic totem of modern culture, lionised by all and prompted by the manufactured celebrity of a few spectacularly talented and lucky individuals, who are anyway part of broader coalitions of enterprise. Rather Paul and John are entrepreneurs as I was once an entrepreneur, as you are or might become: an everyday activity. People fall into and out of this type of activity. Even Schumpeter recognised long ago that engagement with the entrepreneurial role is often a transient one: 'being an entrepreneur is not a profession and as a rule not a lasting condition' ([1934] 1990: 118). Gartner has recognised this too and has asked that enterprise scholars ignore the inner motivations and traits of individuals who create new organisations and focus on what they do (1989: 62). The emphasis on narrative self-identity in this study is perhaps not behaviourist in the manner Gartner suggests, but in showing that narrative resources are mobilised selectively to suit context, this study has added to our understanding of *how* the entrepreneurship role is achieved.

For purist enterprise policy-makers looking for dead cert winners or for scholars that search for the defining traits of the superman, the mundane narratives of people in this book are perhaps redundant or irrelevant: Paul and John can't really be true entrepreneurs, they will say. The enthusiastic erecting of tight fences around small paddocks to my mind closes off the broad reach that enterprise actually has in our lives. Using notions of enterprise to create a sense of self is not the preserve of a few special people, but rather a resource that many use to describe a broad range of activity. Significant voices are now recognising the social and political spread and relevance of enterprise and enterprising behaviour (Gibb 2002; Steyaert and Katz 2004), and the need for different research paradigms in producing knowledge about it (Gartner 1989; Grant and Perren 2002). This study contributes to this deeper and broader sense of enterprise.

Paul and John are, like many, most or all individuals, depending on your view, entrepreneurs of the self as well as people who behave entrepreneurially. Such is the presence of enterprise that we now use it to describe the very manner in which Western selves are created (Giddens 1991; Rose 1996; du Gay 2000b). This has not been my topic. It should be clear that whilst the notion of choice, self-responsibility and reflexivity in crafting a self-narrative are employed in the proceeding pages, and that individuals creatively author the self using a variety of resources, my description and vocabulary rejects the argument that people are totally dominated or constructed by a 'discourse of enterprise'. Paul and John are shaped by discourse, they are immersed in modernity, and they also act and shape their own worlds, their own selves.

Perhaps as a consequence of this emphasis the 'social forces' (Somers 1994: 620) which co-produce the available discourses with which individuals construct narratives appear muted. The theoretical canyons that lie between notions of structure and agency, and the social processes which traverse them, have been skewed towards an individualistic interpretation in this book. I note this as a limitation to the theorising, not a diminution of the empirical contribution. This book is not a work of theory and the discursively pragmatic approach I alluded to in Chapter 2 has acted as friendly guide, rather than a dogmatic set of rules. Thus there has been a tendency for the book to remain focused on 'the entrepreneur' rather than on entrepreneurial processes. If this is a perceived as a failing then avoiding it would have required a far more comprehensive theory of entrepreneurship, or at least a far greater emphasis on developing theory, than has been my purpose.

CONCLUSION

I wrote of Paul and John's relational narratives in Chapter 3 that if their stories hung together too well they might have difficulty convincing themselves and others to believe them: this book is a story, and the same can be said of it. Academic narratives like all texts tend to over-specify their objects of study. Our lust for clarity produces stable, patterned and ordered images of the social world. Producing such clarity in the volume and mess of our inter-subjective and institutional social worlds cannot but be a difficult and combat-like affair, if it is to represent something meaningful. Much of the mental skirmishing that produced my particular story has been fought over the dynamic tension between happenstance and order: between simple arbitrary events and the sensible ordering of episodes.

The themes that I have used to bring each of the chapters into order, and the concluding themes above, should be seen for what they are, part of a conceptual narrative which lusts – however carefully, subtly, reluctantly or poorly – after clarity. The story of this book is not unlike Paul and John's self-identities in the sense that the conceptual narrative I have produced provides a coherent and ordered sense of society. The purpose of this observation is merely to put my hand up and volunteer that this coherence has been created.

As I read through this book I ask the question: is this really the Paul and John I know? I am struck by what has been left out of my story: the emotional attachment I have to Paul, the laughs I had with all of them. My joy, anger: my life. If my self-narrative only plays a cameo part in this story, then Paul and John's stories are similarly partial, though more elaborate: I have only touched on a narrow but substantial part of how they express their self-identities. Taylor puts it well: 'our identity is deeper and more many-sided than any of our possible articulations of it' (1989: 29). Reality is more like the Philip Roth account of knowing other people I quoted at the beginning of this chapter.

Paul and John's lives and self-identities are complex not just in the sense that they amount to more than their work lives, but also in the sense that the stories they tell only refer to a short period of time. As I have said before, things change and continue. Nevertheless, a story needs to end. But this ending too is also an over-specification. The above words should be read bearing in mind this disquiet at the over-specification inherent in committing thoughts and action to text (and especially academic texts, which have institutional as well as textual propensities to neatness).

As with Sennett (1998: 148), Taylor (1991: 103) and Giddens (1991), I do not feel that it is inevitable that our social worlds need to imprison us. Admittedly, my story about Paul and John is not particularly elevating or hopeful in some respects. But this examination of how they have identified, projected and protected themselves does show that within the social institutions we construct and the practices we engage with there *is* room to manoeuvre: room to create meaning, substance, fulfilment and self-realisation. This book has shown that this self-space is not situated and created in a psychic prison or some inner mental world and presented intact and unmediated, but rather through the narratives we tell of ourselves with others. This does not deny thought or biology but connects them to the world about us.

Dan Dennett has begun to popularise a naturalistic version of a narrative view of self, and his recent work (2003) shows that the implications of a biological bodied self, where consciousness and having a self is a virtual and abstract narrative illusion produced via language to facilitate our plans and decision making, does not mean that all is pointless. It really tells us that the emotional, moral, social and cultural worlds we create are more important than what we are made of, how much we weigh and how the machine functions. What we *do* in the worlds we create and inhabit is the real issue.

We create ourselves, and the worlds we live in. And for me this book has also been instrumental in crafting my world and my identity. Personally it represents the culmination of my socialisation into professional academia. This narrative, like Paul and John's, involves choices in a milieu of contextual constraints. Some of the choices I have made in preparing this book, involve me adopting a stance to those socialisation and induction constraints. In particular this has involved me having to deal with translating my lay language into a professional narrative. I have tried hard to retain my everyday sensibilities (although they too have changed over this period as a result of my new everyday experiences) and have written elsewhere (Down 2001a) about why it is a good idea to write in a way that most people can understand. My rationale for this reflects, within these constraints, an attempt to recognise the mutable and moral nature of our engagement with the social world as professional researchers.

Finally then I will close with an observation that Colin Wilson has made. He wrote that 'our identities are like the pane of a window against which we are pressed so tightly that we cannot feel our separateness from it' (Wilson 1978: 280). In talking with and thinking about what Paul and John have said and done, I have tried to create some space between them and the window pane. This book has made the solid but transparent more tangible. Hopefully, in seeing the window pane for what it is, what lies beyond the window is also now held in better perspective: that the relationship between the individual, narrative and their social contexts is clearer and more distinct.

Methodological appendix: writing soap operas[1]

> *No one could agree on anything. We lived in a mist of half-shared, unreliable*
> *perception, and our sense data came warped by a prism of desire and belief,*
> *which tilted our memories too. We saw and remembered in our own favour and*
> *we persuaded ourselves along the way. Pitiless objectivity, especially about*
> *ourselves, was always a doomed social strategy. We're descended from the*
> *indignant, passionate tellers of half truths who in order to convince others,*
> *simultaneously convinced themselves. Over generations success had winnowed*
> *us out, and with success came our defect, carved deep in the genes like ruts in a*
> *cart track – when it suited us we couldn't agree on what was in front of us.*
> *Believing is seeing. That's why there are divorces, border disputes and wars, and*
> *why this statue of the Virgin Mary weeps blood and that one of Ganesh drinks*
> *milk. And that was why metaphysics and science were such courageous*
> *enterprises, such startling inventions, bigger than the wheel, bigger that*
> *agriculture, human artefacts set right against the grain of human nature.*
> *Disinterested truth. But it couldn't save us from ourselves, the ruts were too deep.*
> *There could be no private redemption in objectivity.*
> Ian McEwan *Enduring Love* (1998: 180–181)

INTRODUCTION

What is it about the methods and methodologies used in doing the research at
Fenderco that prompts their relegation to an appendix? This appendix serves
the purpose of clarification and not justification. It is an appendix because it is
of *specialist* interest. There is a need to show one's hand, not in defence of
ethnography as a general mode of inquiry but in regard to the more specific
choices made.

One of the first among these choices was a general orientation to doing
research that saw methods and methodology as means not ends; which is what
they should be. Right from the decision to do the research I wanted it to be as
interesting and meaningful as possible. For me this means I am suspicious of
those that cede too much importance to the prescriptions and rules of research,
over the problems the research is hoping to illuminate. In taking this stance I
have forever joined in with the unruly scrum of pragmatism against the pack
of dogmatists and the 'hegemony of the methodologists' (Ackroyd 1996: 449).
This appendix shows what this stance has meant in practice.

A second purpose is to reaffirm a connection with the experience of doing the research. It has been close on a decade since I first ventured to Maltonbury as a researcher. In writing this book I have worried occasionally about how my experience has been transformed. The story I tell has progressively become a more coherently organised and conceptually orientated one. It seems to have much more of a point to it than it once did, which is clearly a good thing. All forms of narratives need to have the random events of experience filtered and selectively appropriated, and then retold in interesting and useful ways. There is something lost though in this process of ordering and conceptual articulation: something real and earthy and for me particularly attractive and meaningful. This appendix gives something more of that original experience back. It provides some of the notes in the margins: 'The Making of *Narratives of Enterprise*: The Director's Cut.'

A third purpose seeks to add to the analysis, albeit in a specialised manner. All research topics have methodological implications. Unlike some topics however, I work on my self-identities via the same processes that Paul, John, Mark and Will do. We all do. Hence, my presence is also an unavoidable object of research. Not in the hackneyed and moribund sense of polluting otherwise pure research, rather, as an opportunity to extend the study. The reader, having read about how I too would construct self-identity in conversing with Paul and the others, or through the writing of this book, will be able to better assess the manner in which the research was crafted.

These choices are subsumed within a more traditional chronology of ethnographic research: starting with research design and access, collecting information through observation and interviewing, problems and ethical issues in the field, and finally writing concerns.

DOING THE FIELDWORK

I started this book with a little story of when I used to run a record label. This experience of being an entrepreneur of sorts has proved a key self-defining episode of my life. Even my academic interest in enterprise is an aspect of my own quest for self-knowledge. Who was that person? How, why, did he do all that stuff? The occasional e-mails I still receive about my record label, often from people who weren't even born at the time, prompt me to think about who I was back then. The academic artefacts I produce should be seen as stemming from a fascination with the processes of enterprise. I feel entrepreneurial in what I think and do. Along with Paul and John I construct my academic self-identity in opposition to the routine, conservative and bureaucratic institutions around me.

When it came to doing my Warwick masters dissertation in 1994 (eventually published as Down and Bresnen 1997), it seemed obvious and inevitable that I should research small firms and entrepreneurs. Fellow masters student Chris Moule's covert ethnography (1998), my other subsequent research, and studies by Monder Ram (1994) and Ruth Holliday (1995) slowly guided and inspired me towards a desire to undertake ethnographic research in a small firm for my doctoral dissertation. The problem was how to do the research.

Seeing as I already knew Paul and he had already acted as an interviewee (Down and Caldwell 1996), it seemed sensible to talk to him about my proposed doctoral research. It took a little time however to convince myself that having a research site with a friend in situ might be a legitimate way of researching. Even interpretively empathetic colleagues warned of the potential risks, whereas many authors wrote that despite this there were many benefits to the admixture of friendship and research in studying smaller firms (Ram 1994; Hobbs 1988; Moule 1998). Kondo (1990) and Holliday (1995) have shown that friendships are inevitably formed in long-term qualitative research even when they do not pre-date the research itself. One way of achieving thick description is already in some way being part of what is being described. Encouraged by these writers and my supervisor, I asked Paul and the deal was done: the research was on.

Our relationship was always an easy going one. We had first met in the early 1980s. We were both relatively new to London, Paul beginning his career at Harbourco, and myself playing in and managing bands, and packing meat for Debenhams in Oxford Street. We were comfortable and open with each other but were not close friends, and after a short period of living in opposite apartments in a house in Ladbrooke Grove we would meet for a beer every few months: I a fringe player in his clique and he the same in mine. And, with the occasional break, such as his four-year stay in Asia working for EuroPort, this is how our relationship continued until the research started.

My visits to Paul's and other friends in the Maltonbury area were regular even before starting interviewing and taking field notes in early 1997. I would base myself at Paul's 'castle house' and spend the weekend there whilst visiting industrial placement students during the week. This university work continued throughout the research period.

Upon arriving as a researcher therefore, Paul, John and the others were already a regular and normal part of my life. However, it came as something of a jolt to actually start researching. Initially I felt authentic neither as a researcher nor as a friend. My field notes describe the first recorded conversation with Paul as being harder than was expected. They also describe how I was conscious of the potential deleterious effect the whole process might have on our friendship, and how I 'tried to start fairly innocuously, and have skirted some issues. We need to establish our "working" relationship: the limits, style and scope of the conversations'. The awareness therefore, that access is a continually negotiated process (Czarniawska 1998: 33) however strong the researcher/subject bond, was ever present. My reason for being there (as the 'researcher') was something that was continually and implicitly being negotiated.

But there I was. The research was taking place: information was being collected. Two methods were used to collect the words and behaviour contained in this book: recorded and noted conversations, and noted observations. In addition of course, the field notes include my own reflections upon what took place at or near the time.

Observing

Though it was not explicitly discussed in our access 'negotiations' the research was planned knowing that it would not involve continuous and lengthy participant or non-participant observation in the workplace. There were two reasons for this. First, as a full-time lecturer with no opportunity for a sabbatical and with little in the way of specific skills to offer Fenderco in exchange for continuous access it was not possible to reside at the firm. Indeed though I did spend many an hour hanging around in the office – either engaging in small talk, using the office computers, fax, photocopier and so on, or waiting to talk to someone, waiting to drive to a site somewhere, or waiting to go for lunch – actually observing everyday working practices for long enough so that it would produce particularly inspiring material was not feasible. I was not and could not become an insider in the office. Thus, the second reason was as we saw in Chapter 5 that in an open plan office with five people hard at work (buying, selling, drawing plans, telephoning, calculating, thinking and talking) there was little room for a fly on the wall.

When first thinking about the research I had thought that not being able to do continuous observation would be a problem. However, certain authors showed that fieldwork could be far more eclectic and pragmatically assembled. Van Maanen encourages adventurousness and experimentation in the field (1988: 127–30, 139), and suggests that the primacy of 'being there' continuously is no guarantee of avoiding the production of formulaic or atheoretical written research (ibid.: 12). Observation at the office, on site, at Paul's home or socialising in the pub was nevertheless a key aspect of the research.

However, the conceptual emphasis on what Paul and John say about themselves in interviews and conversation precludes a dominant observational component. For example, whilst it would have been good to have made more real time observation of generational encounters, this aspect of self-identity is more readily accessible in conversation about past events, situations and decisions: it happens naturally in the spoken rationalisations of action (Giddens 1976: 156).

For those that see qualitative research as a mirror of reality, or a window on the truth, the danger that accounts of the past will be coloured by current circumstances is a real concern. Because this research is interested in self-identity this so-called danger is exactly the point: identity is a narrative of the past, and identity formation is an inherently temporal process. It is what they think, rather than know, about the past and how they articulate it that is important.

My observations do serve to confirm what is said, such as when I saw the different moods that would pervade the Fenderco office. More interestingly the observed material would often provide an alternative version to the talked about sense of themselves they present in the interviews, such as the change that Paul and John underwent when going on site.

Neither the talking self nor the observed self holds any privileged representation to a true self. Being present and observing provided me with a way of both building relationships and as a way of checking my understanding of what was going on. Thus, whilst I did not write down or capture all the words and conversations seen and heard in the office, of an evening over dinner at Paul's home, or in the pub, my natural social sensibilities and the 'mutual knowledge' (Giddens 1976: 161) I share with them must have mixed and cross-referenced with my reflections about the research, checking whether my impressions from inside the research were consistent with those from outside.

Interviewing

The recorded interviews with Paul, John, Mark and Will took place in a variety of settings: Paul's home, Mark's home in an extended lunch break, in John's office and so on. Though access was agreed actually pinning people down proved harder in practice. Whilst staying in Maltonbury I would often walk to the Fenderco office and find that the intended interviewee was not there or was busy. I therefore had to be fairly flexible and 'entrepreneurial' (Ram 2000: 657; Hobbs 1988: 7) and take my opportunities as they arose.

The conversations were open and wide-ranging. There was no specific structure to the conversations beyond those culturally ascribed conventions common to all social interaction and a guiding sense of what is and is not interesting. But as Burgess has noted this does not mean that they were conversation without purpose (1982: 107). The conversations with the owner-managers were generally structured in terms of a chronology of their relationship to each other and the history of their careers. The conversations with Mark and Will were explicitly focused towards their understandings of and relationships with, the owner-managers.

The process of spending time and sitting down with individuals had some interesting effects. The interview changed relationships. Will's attitude to me changed considerably after our interview. In The Grinning Cat pub later that week he now spoke to me about his upbringing and personal trials and tribulations. As I stated in my field notes: 'It was as though the interview had been a confession, and now we have a bond'. The process of sitting down, one-to-one, and doing the interview seemed to draw myself closer to all.

Despite the importance of interview material in this study, like all methods it is not unproblematic. Paradoxically, though interviewing is now widely accepted even by those philosophically unsympathetic to qualitative methodologies (hence the rise of the quantitative frequency-based approach to interview data), recently a critique of the interview has emerged (Alvesson and Kärreman 2000; Atkinson and Silverman 1997). The automatic and assumed authenticity of the interview is now questioned: as Burgess put it, 'how do we know the informant is telling the truth?' (1982: 109).

Happily the interview data in this book is not being presented as truth (except of course in that it is not made-up! – on the validity of even this, see Watson 2000). What is represented by the interview materials are self-identity narratives that Paul, John and myself have jointly produced. Atkinson and Silverman argue that the form of the interview is embedded so deeply into our society that 'the self is rehearsed' for the interview (1997: 314). The initial difficulties I experienced in interviewing Paul were I think, partly due to the mutual sense of embarrassment and amusement at taking on the roles of interviewer and interviewee.[2] The interviews were part of how Paul, the others and I produced self-identity: less a method for ascertaining the truth than a vehicle for producing it.

This can be seen in more detail in an excerpt from a conversation with Paul. It was around 10pm and the interview had finished. We were about to pop down the pub for last orders and our conversation turned towards our mutual experience of being entrepreneurs: the tape recorder was turned on again and Paul said

There are very few people that I have worked with and for that are prepared to take that risk to run their own business. And that's what sets entrepreneurs above employees (most of them), for most ... for many people their personal objective is the security of having a job and not wanting to put anything on the line ... [pause] ... *the responsibility and effort ... [pause]. As you know, despite being really far too young and not having any business sense or anything [when I ran my record company], I do know basically, more or less what it's like [to be an entrepreneur] and I suspect that in the future I may well ... [pause]. I don't know if I have ever told you that I was chatting to my boss after the end of the first year [of working in academia] and I asked her 'what do you envisage me doing in the future?' and she said she 'could see me running my own research company', you know ... I hate being an employee.*

It's [being an entrepreneur] obviously within you. You have done it before and it's part of your psyche, it's there and it may come back one day.

In this slice of conversation we are both constructing and identifying our biographical narratives with the mutually desired 'character' of the entrepreneur: we are producing this particular sense of ourselves.

This conversation raises interesting questions about the identity self-management of the researcher (Czarniawska 1998). Was I constructing a 'true' sense of my self when talking of possibly working as an entrepreneur in the future? To what extent was I managing or performing my identity *or* my research? I honestly don't know. It is no 'truer' about my own self-identity than a conversation I might have now with an academic colleague about being a particular type of academic. Neither my authorial voice nor Paul and John's voices have any inherent authenticity. The voices do tell us something, but they need to be pragmatically accepted, not seen as truth.

FRIENDSHIP, RESEARCH AND SELF-IDENTITY

All research where people are the subjects involves the investigator adopting certain roles, behaviours and projecting certain identities. Hobbs for example writes of managing his image through the clothes he wore being an important aspect of his fieldwork. He also wrote that 'if life was entrepreneurial and sharp, then so would I be. Sexist and chauvinistic, no problem. Racist? Well, no' (1988: 11). Similarly, I also had choices to make about how to *be*: what identity to adopt. Throughout the period of the research I felt that the very nature of talking to and observing people with a 'purpose' in mind, and thinking academically about what was done and said (that is, being a researcher), somehow involved me being inauthentic; a covert participant. I don't mean that I did not talk about my interests with my informants, or that I misled them. But this self-conscious feeling was nevertheless pervasive. An example of this reflexive tension in conducting research can be seen below in the dialectic between my identities as friend and researcher.

Midway during the research Paul began experiencing difficulties in his marriage. I was involved both as a friend of his wife and more specifically as a friend and confidant of Paul. These difficulties also had their effect on the fieldwork. One visit to Maltonbury for instance when he was particularly preoccupied with work and these difficulties, 'produced no talk with Paul' (from field notes, meaning an extended recorded or noted conversation). On one particular evening in The Grinning Cat the tensions between being friends with both Paul and his wife overflowed into a frank exchange of views and a disagreement about the nature and scope of our friendship and the level of involvement in each other's affairs. The issue of the research was not raised in the conversation. Though not especially dramatic in itself, this event did mark something of a significant change in the nature of our relationship. I was aware, as this extract from my notes shows, of the impact these tensions were having on the conduct of the research

> The whole thing [Paul's marriage problems and their effect on our friendship] is a problem with regards the research, as I am in a sense too close to the subject. Now, whilst this presents advantages, the whole project is subject to the ebbs and flows of my relationship with Paul. […]. The point is that maybe we are too close? […]. There are some things which impinge upon the research which are not necessarily the proper subject of inquiry. Can the research carry on under these circumstances? Where do I draw the line?

Like Hobbs, who drew a line between being sexist and being racist in the entrepreneurial pursuit of his research I too drew a line between being a friend and being a researcher in this particular incident. For most of the time the edge between these identities was happily indistinct and comfortably accommodated in the confusion and intimacies of everyday life, but for me on this particular evening the boundary was clearly delineated. These tensions between the identities of researcher and friend are a problem of the tension between my sense of who and how to be. The me that is a friend was ultimately in this particular instance more important to me than the me at work. The research did carry on, productively and for some time, though ultimately this change in our relationship meant that the fieldwork was cut short.

These issues remain unresolved for me both as researcher and friend. When I next went into the field, at the coke ovens of a steel works in Wollongong, Australia (Down et al. 2003), I sought to maintain more of a distance. The 'emotional investment' (Hobbs 1988: 10) that is made in research raises difficult personal, professional and epistemological issues. From a personal point of view I would rather not have to deal with these issues so profoundly again. The issues of my identities – as entrepreneur, friend and researcher – have featured occasionally in the story of Fenderco, but the topic of this book is the processes of self-identity construction and maintenance of two entrepreneurs.

My relative absence from the story is also because there are some legitimate limits to what can be told.

LIMITS TO THE TELLING

Thus, whilst my reflexivity is important as it recognises that I am part of what is being studied, this does not mean that I should tell the reader everything about my life. This is a confessional ethnography about self-identity in a small organisation setting not 'a black hole of introspection' (Van Maanen 1988: 92). This book is framed by a concern with organisational issues (small firms, entrepreneurial identity, work and so on) and is therefore inherently limited.

However, being part of what is being studied means that other aspects of my informant's lives were seen, heard and noted. But the details of Paul's marriage cannot constitute part of the analysis. The main reasons for this are because it is not *as* relevant as what was considered, selected and presented (Becker 1986b). Importantly, it would also not be decent to do so. Some boundaries are placed around our experience as researchers. An aspect of these boundaries includes my own emotional investment and sense of loyalty to the people of this study.

There is another limit to the telling. There is as Philip Roth and Ian McEwan both recognise, also the limit to what one *can* possibly know about other people. At one point in the fieldwork for instance, after his marital difficulties became apparent, Paul suggested to me that he might 'break with Fenderco in the not too distant future'. This comment came as something of a surprise given the way Paul usually talked of the company's continuing success and grand future, and it raised paranoid doubts in my mind about what I really knew about what was going on, as well as the obligatory selfish fears about continuing access! At the time in my field notes I wrote, 'He seems to be suggesting that he will break with Fenderco in the not too distant future. Might it be that there are more substantial problems existing in the company? How do I *know* what is going on? What do I consider legitimate and illegitimate information? Questions, questions ...' In this sense the data I have collected, in terms of what it or any data can tell about self-identity, reminds me of what barristers have to contend with in constructing their narratives about past events. Court evidence is never complete, and can ignore facts deemed illegitimate under certain legal criteria. Different interpretations and theories are also made using the same facts. Qualitative research materials however exhaustive or comprehensive are the same: there is always something that is left out. Ultimately, it depends on the story one wishes to tell and who your audience is.

ENDING THE RESEARCH?

The last research visit to Maltonbury took place in November 1998. It was then that I realised that I was not willing to continue and complete the planned research. The original research design had ambitiously planned for three stages, which in addition to punctuated interviewing and observation of the owner-managers and employees (stage one and two) would include interviews with the 'wider personal, social and commercial networks' (Down 1999a: 277) of the owner-managers.

My field notes from this visit explain that the combination of Paul's continuing marriage difficulties and the tensions in our friendship meant that 'I have lost the enthusiasm [for the research], and [thus also] in a sense the "access": this in the sense that I am not really part of the organisation now'. Nothing particularly dramatic had occurred. There had been no censure or closing of the gates. Paul had even agreed that I could make appointments to see his solicitor and accountant as a first foray into stage three of the research. Subsequent discussions with Paul some time after the research had finished suggested that though he was aware of the change in my attitude to him, he was generally unaware as to what had caused it. But I had had enough. I was also sufficiently excited about the data that had already been collected to think that I had enough to be going on with.

In some limited sense though, the fieldwork didn't stop at all. My relationship with Paul and the others had changed and I was not engaged with these people as a researcher any longer. Paul and I were still friends (though the relationship had changed). I still visited Maltonbury. I still talked with them about Fenderco and my research, but I had stopped being the 'researcher', taking notes and looking for meaning (well as much as I could; I may have stopped taking notes, but it is a very different matter to stop thinking, especially when Fenderco continued to provide the main context of my research work). I was just me again: the friend, acquaintance and one of those 'fucking academics who don't know anything about the real world', to quote Will.

Despite my enthusiasm for the concepts I was developing from my data analysis, disappointment hung over the fieldwork like one of those personalised cartoon rain clouds, following me around. In a sense my wiser, older, more conservative colleagues had been right about the risks of combining friendship and fieldwork. As life, teaching, conference papers (Down and Sadler-Smith 1999), and other research work (Down 1999b) trundled on, and as the fieldwork experience slipped away into memory and narrative construction, I was able to feel more confident about what I had achieved: what I found in the data inspired, fascinated and importantly kept me working.

RESEARCH AS WRITING AND CONSTRUCTING IDENTITY

Work for academics means writing. It is appropriate therefore to conclude with some reflections on that process.

What has impressed me writing all these years about Fenderco is how important a vehicle it has become in constructing my own sense of self. The reading, writing and referencing conventions of academia do more than provide a common base on which to create knowledge or facilitate scholarly conversations (Czarniawska 1998). They are also the equipment of professional socialisation: they form our rules of expression and a guide to appropriate behaviour. The influences on my writing style and the citations I use are the locating evidence of that socialisation. Writing is important and the story I tell is ultimately a piece of writing more than it is a piece of fieldwork.

The craft of academic writing also forms a narrative environment for the production of my own career identity. What type of academic I want to and can be, and the meaning this has for my own narrative of self. Just as Paul and John talk the talk of the entrepreneurial clichéd narrative in constructing their identities, I write the text of a certain type of academic. The crafting of this book and my own career more generally has created a space in which I have consolidated the disparate elements of events of my own biography into a secure and effective self-identity. In particular I have sort to consolidate the entrepreneurial together with the academic narratives. Though my activities as independent record label owner, meatpacker, London Underground worker, student and academic might seem fragmented, the narrative which I have constructed, am constructing here, is of a piece. Even my academic interests in small firms, work and organisations are the consequence of the narrative crafted from the events of my life.

I could go on. I did not intend this work to have such personal meaning. Untangling the narrative threads that make up our own lives is arguably harder than looking at others. As relative ignorance produces clarity, honesty and a good memory this surely does no favours in understanding our own narratives. Thankfully my task has been to tell a story about others, I hope it has been an interesting one.

NOTES

1. One of my supervisors, Eugene Sadler-Smith, asked me early in the fieldwork, when I would return to my office enthusing about my experiences: 'Was your aim to write a research project or a soap opera?' (Down and Sadler-Smith 1999: 15). For some time neither of us was too sure about the answer.
2. Eventually however we seemed to incorporate this new dialogue into the modus operandi of our relationship. The amusement and embarrassment soon evaporated from our conversation, replaced for me by a workaday sense of fieldwork being achieved, and for Paul a sense of an opportunity to talk about and reflect upon his project of Fenderco and his life more generally. Undoubtedly this new context for our relationship changed its nature, especially in the extent to which Paul's career activity became the predominant topic of conversation. But the mutual exploration of our careers had always provided a central focus of our friendship anyway.

References

Ackroyd, S. (1996), 'The quality of qualitative methods: qualitative or quality methodology for organisation studies?', *Organization*, **3**(3): 439–51.

Ackroyd, S. and Thompson, P. (1999), *Organizational* Mis*behaviour*, London, UK and Thousand Oaks, US: Sage.

Alvesson, M. (1994), 'Talking in organizations: managing identity and impressions in an advertising agency', *Organization Studies*, **15**(4): 535–63.

Alvesson, M. (1995), 'The meaning and meaninglessness of postmodernism: some ironic remarks', *Organization Studies*, **16**(6): 1047–75.

Alvesson, M. and Kärreman, D. (2000), 'Taking the linguistic turn in organizational research: challenges, responses, consequences', *Journal of Applied Behavioural Science*, **36**(2): 136–58.

Alvesson, M. and Willmott, H. (2002), 'Identity regulation as organizational control: producing the appropriate individual', *Journal of Management Studies*, **39**(5): 619–44.

Anderson-Gough, F., Grey, C. and Robson, K. (1998) '"Work hard, play hard": an analysis of organizational cliché in two accountancy practices', *Organization*, **5**(4): 565–92.

Archer, M., Bhaskar, R., Collier, A., Lawson, T. and Norrie, A. (1998), *Critical Realism: Essential Readings*, London, UK and New York, US: Routledge.

Argyris, C. and Schon, D.A. (1974), *Theory in Practice: Increasing Professional Effectiveness*, San Francisco: Jossey-Bass.

Atkinson, P. and Silverman, D. (1997), 'Kundera's immortality: the interview society and the invention of the self', *Qualitative Inquiry*, **3**(3): 304–25.

Bagnall, N. (1985), *A Defence of Clichés*, London: Constable.

Beck, U. (2000), *The Brave New World of Work*, Cambridge: Polity Press.

Becker, H. and Hill Useem, R. (1942), 'Sociological analysis of the dyad', *American Sociological Review*, **7**: 13–26.

Becker, H.S. (1963), *Outsiders: Studies in the Sociology of Deviance*, London, UK and Chicago, US: University of Chicago Press.

Becker, H.S. (1986a), *Writing for Social Scientists: How to Start and Finish your Thesis, Book, or Article*, London, UK and Chicago, US: University of Chicago Press.

Becker, H.S. (1986b), *Doing Things Together*, Evanston: Northwestern University Press.

Bendle, M.F. (2002), 'The crisis of "identity" in high modernity', *British Journal of Sociology*, **53**(1): 1–18.

Berger, P.L. and Luckmann, T. ([1965]1991), *The Social Construction of Reality: A Treatise in the Sociology of Knowledge*, London, UK and New York, US: Penguin.

Bessant, J., Birley, S., Cooper, C., Dawson, S., Gennard J., Gardiner, M., Gray, A., Jones, P., Mayer, J., McGee, J., Pidd, M., Rowley, G., Saunders, J. and Stark, A. (2003), 'The state of the field in UK management research: reflections of the research assessment exercise (RAE) panel', *British Journal of Management*, **14**(1): 51–68.

Boden, D. and Molotch, H.L. (1994), 'The compulsion of proximity', in R. Friedland and D. Boden (eds), *NowHere: Space, Time and Modernity*, Berkeley: University of California Press, pp. 257–86.

Bourdieu, P. (1977), *An Outline of a Theory of Practice*, Cambridge, UK and New York, US: Cambridge University Press.

Bourdieu, P. (1985), 'The social space and the genesis of groups', *Theory and Society*, **14**: 723–44.

Brubaker, R. and Cooper, F. (2000), 'Beyond "identity"', *Theory and Society*, **29**(1): 1–47.

Brunsson, N. (1985), *The Irrational Organization. Irrationality as a Basis for Organizational Action and Change*, New York: Wiley.

Burgess, R. (ed.) (1982), *Field Research, a Source Book and Field Manual*, London: Allen and Unwin.

Burkitt, I. (1994), 'The shifting concept of the self', *History of the Human Sciences*, **7**(2): 7–28.

Burrell, G. and Morgan, G. (1979), *Sociological Paradigms and Organisational Analysis: Elements of the Sociology of Corporate Life*, London: Heinemann.

Burrows, R. (1991), 'Introduction: entrepreneurship, petty capitalism and the restructuring of Britain', in R. Burrows (ed.), *Deciphering the Enterprise Culture: Entrepreneurship, Petty Capitalism and the Restructuring of Britain*, London, UK and New York, US: Routledge, pp. 1–16.

Burrows, R. and Curran, J. (1989), 'Sociological research on service sector small businesses: some conceptual considerations', *Work Employment and Society*, **3**(4): 527–39.

Bygrave, W.D. (1989), 'The entrepreneurship paradigm (I): a philosophical look at its research methodologies', *Entrepreneurship, Theory and Practice*, **14**: 7–26.

Casey, C. (1995), *Work, Self and Society: After Industrialism*, London, UK and New York, US: Routledge.

Chambers Dictionary, The (1994), Edinburgh: Chambers Harrap Publishers.

Chell, E., Haworth, J.M. and Brearly, S. (1991), *The Entrepreneurial*

Personality: Concepts, Case and Categories, London, UK and New York, US: Routledge.

Cohen, L. and Musson, G. (2000), 'Entrepreneurial identities: reflections from two case studies', *Organization*, 7(1): 31–48.

Cohen, S. and Taylor, L. (1992), *Escape Attempts: The Theory and Practice of Resistance to Everyday Life*, London, UK and New York, US: Routledge.

Collinson, D. (1992), *Managing the Shopfloor: Subjectivity, Masculinity and Workplace Culture*, Berlin: de Gruyter.

Corsten, M. (1999), 'The time of generations', *Time and Society*, 8(2): 249–72.

Curran, J. (1986), 'The survival of the petite bourgeoisie: production and reproduction', in J. Curran, J. Stanworth, and D. Watkins (eds), *The Survival of the Small Firm 2: Employment, Growth, Technology and Politics*, Aldershot: Gower, pp. 204–27.

Curran, J. (1990), 'Rethinking economic structure: exploring the role of the small firm and self-employment in the British economy', *Work, Employment and Society*, additional special issue May: 125–46.

Curran, J. and Blackburn, R.A. (eds) (1991), *Paths of Enterprise: The Future of the Small Business*, London, UK and New York, US: Routledge.

Curran, J. and Blackburn, R.A. (1994), *Small Firms and Local Economic Networks: The Death of the Local Economy*, London: Paul Chapman.

Curran, J. and Burrows, R. (1987), 'Ethnographic approaches to the study of the small business owner', in K. O'Neill, R. Bhambri, T. Faulkner and T. Cannon (eds), *Small Business Development*, Aldershot: Avebury, pp. 3–24.

Curran, J. and Stanworth, J. (1979), 'Worker involvement and social relations in the small firm', *The Sociological Review*, 27(2): 317–42.

Curran, J. and Stanworth, J. (1984), 'Small business research in Britain', in C. Levicki (ed.), *Small Business: Europe*, Beckenham: Croom Helm.

Czarniawska, B. (1998), *A Narrative Approach to Organization Studies*, London, UK and Thousand Oaks, US: Sage.

Davies, B. and Harré, R. (1991), 'Positioning: the discursive production of selves', *Journal for the Theory of Social Behaviour*, 20(1): 43–63.

Davis, M.S. (1971), 'That's interesting! Towards a phenomenology of sociology and sociology of phenomenology, *Philosophy of Social Science*, I: 309–34.

Davis, M.S. (1999), 'Aphorisms and clichés: the generation and dissipation of conceptual charisma', *Annual Review of Sociology*, 25: 245–69.

Dennett, D.C. (1982), 'Comments on Rorty', *Synthese*, 53: 349–56.

Dennett, D.C. (1993), *Consciousness Explained*, London: Penguin.

Dennett, D.C. (2003), *Freedom Evolves*, London: Penguin.

Derrida, J. (2000), 'Différance', in P. du Gay, J. Evans and P. Redman (eds), *Identity: A Reader*, London, UK and Thousand Oaks, US: Sage, pp. 87–93.

Dibben, M.R. (2000), *Exploring Interpersonal Trust in the Entrepreneurial Venture*, Basingstoke: MacMillan.

Dick, B. and Morgan, G. (1987), 'Family networks and employment in textiles', *Work, Employment and Society*, **1**: 225–46.

Down, S. (1999a), 'Owner-manager learning in small firms', *Journal of Small Business and Enterprise Development*, **6**(3): 267–80.

Down, S. (1999b), '(Yet) another side of HRM?', *Organization*, **6**(3): 543–60.

Down, S. (2001a), 'The return of popular social science?', *Human Relations*, **54**(12): 1639–62.

Down, S. (2001b), 'The use of history in business and management, and some implications for management learning', *Management Learning*, **32**(3): 395–417.

Down, S. (2001c), 'Review of M. Dibben (2000) *Exploring Interpersonal Trust in the Entrepreneurial Venture*', *Journal of Management Studies*, **38**(5): 753–6.

Down, S. (2002), 'Clichés, generations, space and friendship: the self-identity narratives of two entrepreneurs', unpublished Ph.D. Thesis, University of Wollongong, Australia.

Down, S. and Bresnen, M. (1997), 'The impact of training enterprise councils on the provision of small business support: case studies in London and the Midlands', *Local Economy*, **11**(4): 317–32.

Down, S. and Caldwell, N. (1996), '"Faking" it in supply chain relationships?', paper presented at Manufacturing Matters, Employment Research Unit Conference, Cardiff Business School. Abstract published in *Management Research News*, **20**(2/3): 55–6.

Down, S. and Reveley, J. (2004), 'Generational encounters and the social formation of entrepreneurial identity – "young guns" and "old farts"', *Organization*, **11**(2): 233–50.

Down, S. and Sadler-Smith, E. (1999), '"Covertness", friendship and subjectivity in research: a plea for more realism, openness and relevance in academic dialogue', paper presented at Taking Liberties, Standing Conference on Organisational Symbolism, Edinburgh, July.

Down, S., Badham, R. and Garrety, K. (2003), 'Clichés of resistance: some irreverent thoughts, doubts, and questions about resistance in contemporary culture change programs and organisations more generally', paper presented at APROS, Mexico.

du Gay, P. (2000a), 'Enterprises and its futures: a response to Fournier and Grey', *Organization*, **7**(1): 165–83.

du Gay, P. (2000b), *In Praise of Bureaucracy, Weber, Organization, Ethics*, London, UK and Thousand Oaks, US: Sage.

Eco, U. (2002), *Baudolino*, London: Secker and Warburg.

Erikson, E.H. (1968), *Identity, Youth and Crisis*, New York: W.W. Norton.

Flaubert, G. (1975), *Madame Bovary*, London, UK and New York, US: Penguin.

Fletcher, D. (2003) 'Framing organizational emergence: discourse, identity and relationship', in D. Hjorth and C. Steyaert (eds), *New Movements in Entrepreneurship*, Cheltenham, UK and Northampton, MA, US: Edward Elgar, pp. 125–42.

Foucault, M. (1982), 'Afterword: the subject and power', in H.L. Dreyfus and P. Rabinow (eds), *Michel Foucault: Beyond Structuralism and Hermeneutics*, Hemel Hempstead: Harvester Press, pp. 208–26.

Fournier, V. and Grey, C. (1999), 'Too much, too little and too often: a critique of du Gay's analysis of enterprise', *Organization*, **6**(1): 107–28.

Gartner, W.B. (1989) '"Who is an entrepreneur?" Is the wrong question', *Entrepreneurship Theory and Practice*, Summer: 47–67.

Geertz, C. (1973), *The Interpretation of Cultures*, New York: Basic Books.

Gergen, K.J. (1978), 'Towards generative theory', *Journal of Personality and Social Psychology*, **36**(11): 1344–60.

Gibb, A. (2002) 'In pursuit of a new "enterprise" and "entrepreneurship" paradigm for learning: creative destruction, new values, new ways of doing things and new combinations of knowledge', *International Journal of Management Reviews*, **4**(3): 233–70.

Giddens, A. (1976), *New Rules of Sociological Method* (first edn), London: Hutchinson.

Giddens, A. (1984), *The Constitution of Society: Outline of the Theory of Structuration*, Cambridge: Polity Press.

Giddens, A. (1991), *Modernity and Self-identity: Self and Society in the Late Modern Age*, Cambridge: Polity Press.

Giddens, A. (1992), *The Transformation of Intimacy: Sexuality, Love and Eroticism in Modern Societies*, Cambridge: Polity Press.

Giddens, A. (1993), *New Rules of Sociological Method* (second edn), Cambridge: Polity Press.

Gillett, G. (1999) 'Dennett, Foucault, and the selection of memes', *Inquiry*, **43**(3): 2–23.

Goffman, E. ([1959]1990), *The Presentation of Self in Everyday Life*, London, UK and New York, US: Penguin.

Goffman, E. (1961), *Asylums*, New York: Anchor.

Goffman, E. (1968), *Stigma: Notes on the Management of Spoiled Identity*, London, UK and New York, US: Pelican Books.

Goffman, E. (1971), *Relations in Public: Microstudies of the Public Order*, New York: Basic Books.

Goffman, E. (1972), *Encounters: Two Studies in the Sociology of Interaction*, London: The Penguin Press.

Goss, D. (1991), *Small Business and Society*, London, UK and New York, US:

Routledge.

Grant, P. and Perren, L. (2002), 'Small business and entrepreneurial research: meta-theories, paradigms and prejudices', *International Small Business Journal*, **20**(2): 185–211.

Gray, C. (1998), *Enterprise and Culture*, London, UK and New York, US: Routledge.

Gray, J. (2003), *Straw Dogs: Thoughts on Humans and Other Animals*, London: Granta.

Hall, S. (2000), 'Who needs "identity"', in P. du Gay, J. Evans and P. Redman (eds), *Identity: A Reader*, London, UK and Thousand Oaks, US: Sage, pp. 15–30.

Hendry, J. (2004), *Between Enterprise and Ethics: Business and Management in a Bimoral Society*, Oxford: Oxford University Press.

Hjorth, D. and Steyaert, C. (eds) (2004) *Narrative and Discursive Approaches in Entrepreneurship*, Cheltenham, UK and Northampton, MA, US: Edward Elgar.

Hobbs, D. (1988), *Doing the Business: Entrepreneurship, the Working Class, and Detectives in the East End of London*, Oxford: Clarendon Press.

Holliday, R. (1995), *Investigating Small Firms: Nice Work?*, London, UK and New York, US: Routledge.

Hughes, G. (1988), *Words in Time: A Social History of the English Vocabulary*, Oxford: Blackwell.

Hunt, G. and Satterlee, S. (1986), 'The pub, the village and the people', *Human Organization*, **45**: 62–74.

Jenkins, R. (1996), *Social Identity*, London, UK and New York, US: Routledge.

Kärreman, D. and Alvesson, M. (2001), 'Making newsmakers: conversational identity at work', *Organizational Studies*, **22**(1): 59–89.

Keat, R. and Abercrombie, N. (1990), *Enterprise Culture*, London, UK and New York, US: Routledge.

Kets de Vries, M. (1977), 'The entrepreneurial personality: a person at the crossroads', *Journal of Management Studies*, **14**(1): 34–57.

Kondo, D.K. (1990), *Crafting Selves: Power, Gender, and Discourses of Identity in a Japanese Workplace*, Chicago: University of Chicago Press.

Lave, J. and Wenger, E. (1991), *Situated Learning: Legitimate Peripheral Participation*, Cambridge, UK and New York, US: Cambridge University Press.

Lefebvre, H. (1994), *The Production of Space*, Oxford, UK and Cambridge, MA, US: Blackwell.

Lewis, J.D. and Weigert, A.J. (1981), 'The structures and meanings of social time', *Social Forces*, **60**(2): 432–62.

Lewis, Y. (2003), 'The self as a moral concept', *The British Journal of Social*

Psychology, **42**: 225–37.

Littunen, H. (2000), 'Entrepreneurship and the characteristics of the entrepreneurial personality', *International Journal of Entrepreneurial Behaviour and Research*, **6**(6): 295–303.

Low, M.B. and MacMillan, I.C. (1998), 'Entrepreneurship: past research and future challenges', *Journal of Management*, **35**: 139–61.

MacIntyre, A. (1981), *After Virtue: A Study in Moral Theory*, London: Duckworth.

Mannheim, K. ([1928]1952), *Essays on the Sociology of Knowledge*, London, UK and New York, US: Routledge and Kegan Paul.

McArthur, T. (ed.) (1992), *The Oxford Companion to the English Language*, Oxford: Oxford University Press.

McClelland, D.C. (1961), *The Achieving Society*, New York: D. Van Norstrand.

McEwan, I. (1998), *Enduring Love*, London: Vintage.

Mills, C.W. ([1959]2000), *The Sociological Imagination*, Oxford: Oxford University Press.

Mitchell, R.K., Busenitz, L., Lant, T., McDougall, P.P., Morse, E.A. and Brock Smith, J. (2002), 'Towards a theory of entrepreneurial cognition: Rethinking the people side of entrepreneurship research', *Entrepreneurship, Theory and Practice*, **27**(2): 93–104.

Moule, C. (1998), 'Regulation of work in small firms: a view from the inside', *Work, Employment and Society*, **12**(4): 635–53.

Ogbor, J.O. (2000), 'Mythicizing and reification in entrepreneurial discourse: ideology-critique of entrepreneurial studies', *Journal of Management Studies*, **37**(5): 605–35.

Paine, R. (1970), 'Anthropological approaches to friendship', *Humanitas*, **VI**(2):139–60.

Parker, M. (2000), *Organizational Culture and Identity: Unity and Division at Work*, London, UK and Thousand Oaks, US: Sage.

Partridge, E. ([1940]1979), *A Dictionary of Clichés*, London: Routledge and Kegan Paul.

Potter, J. and Wetherell, M. (1987), *Discourse and Social Psychology: Beyond Attitudes and Behaviour*, London, UK and Thousand Oaks, US: Sage.

Ram, M. (1994), *Managing to Survive: Working Lives in Small Firms*, Oxford: Blackwell.

Ram, M. (2000), 'Hustling, hassling and making it happen: researching consultants in a small firm context', *Organization*, **7**(4): 657–77.

Ram, M. and Holliday, R. (1993), 'Relative merits: family culture and kinship in small firms', *Sociology*, **27**(4): 629–48.

Reed, M.I. (1997), 'In praise of duality and dualism: rethinking agency and structure in organizational analysis', *Organization Studies*, **18**(1): 21–42.

Reed, M.I. (1998), 'Organizational analysis as discourse analysis: a critique', in D. Grant, T. Keenoy and C. Oswick (eds), *Discourse and Organization*, London, UK and Thousand Oaks, US: Sage, pp. 193–213.

Reed, M.I. (2000), 'The limits of discourse analysis in organizational analysis', *Organization*, **7**(3): 524–30.

Reveley, J., Down, S. and Taylor, S. (2004), 'Beyond the boundaries: an ethnographic analysis of spatially diffuse control in a small firm', *International Small Business Journal*, **22**(4): 349–67.

Reynolds P. (1991), 'Sociology and entrepreneurship: concepts and contributions', *Entrepreneurship Theory and Practice*, **16**(2): 47–70.

Rorty, R. (1982), 'Comments on Dennett', *Synthese*, **53**: 181–7.

Rorty, R. (1989), *Contingency, Irony, and Solidarity*, Cambridge, UK and New York, US: Cambridge University Press.

Rose, N. (1996), *Inventing our Selves: Psychology, Power, and Personhood*, Cambridge, UK and New York, US: Cambridge University Press.

Roth, P. (1998), *American Pastoral*, London: Vintage.

Rotter, J.B., Chance, J.E. and Phares, E.J. (1972), *Applications of a Social Learning Theory of Personality*, New York: Holt, Rinehart & Winston.

Rubin, L.B. (1985), *Just Friends: The Role of Friendship in Our Lives*, New York: Harper & Row.

Sartre, J.P. (1973), *Existentialism and Humanism*, London: Eyre Methuen.

Scase, R. and Goffee, R. (1980), *The Real World of the Small Business Owner*, London: Croom Helm.

Schumpeter, J.A. [1934 (1990)], 'The theory of economic development', in *An Inquiry Into Profits, Capital, Credit, Interest and the Business Cycle*, Cambridge, MA: Harvard University Press, pp. 64–94, reprinted in M. Casson (ed.) (1990), *Entrepreneurship*, Aldershot, UK and Brookfield, US: Edward Elgar, pp. 105–34.

Sennett, R. (1974), *The Fall of Public Man*, Cambridge: Cambridge University Press.

Sennett, R. (1981), *Authority*, New York: Vintage Books.

Sennett, R. (1998), *The Corrosion of Character: The Personal Consequences of Work in the New Capitalism*, New York: Norton.

Sennett, R. (2000), 'Street and office: two sources of identity', in W. Hutton and A. Giddens (eds), *On the Edge: Living with Global Capitalism*, London: Jonathan Cape, pp. 175–90.

Shapero, A. and Sokol, L. (1982), 'The social dimensions of entrepreneurship', in C. Kent, D. Sexton and K. Vesper (eds), *Encyclopedia of Entrepreneurship*, Englewood Cliffs: Prentice-Hall, pp. 72–90.

Shapin, S. (2001), 'Proverbial economies: how an understanding of some linguistic and social features of common sense can throw light on more prestigious bodies of knowledge, science for example', *Social Studies of*

Science, **31**(5): 731–69.

Silverman, D. (1970), *The Theory of Organisations: A Sociological Framework*, London: Heinemann.

Somers, M.R. (1994), 'The narrative constitution of identity: a relational and network approach', *Theory and Society*, **23**: 605–49.

Stanworth, J. and Curran, J. (1984), 'Small business research in Britain', in C. Levicki (ed.), *Small Business: Europe*, Beckenham: Croom Helm, pp. 127–52.

Steyaert, C. and Katz, J. (2004), 'Reclaiming the space of entrepreneurship in society: geographical, discursive and social dimensions', *Entrepreneurship and Regional Development*, **16**: 179–96.

Storey, D. and Sykes, N. (1996), 'Uncertainty, innovation and management', in P. Burns and J. Dewhurst (eds), *Small Business and Entrepreneurship* (second edn), London: MacMillan, pp. 73–93.

Strauss, A.L. (1959), *Mirrors and Masks: The Search for Identity*, Illinois: Free Press of Glencoe.

Taylor, C. (1989), *Sources of the Self: The Making of the Modern Identity*, Cambridge, MA, Harvard University Press.

Taylor, C. (1991), *The Ethics of Authenticity*, Cambridge, MA: Harvard University Press.

Tsoukas, H. (2000), 'False dilemmas in organization theory: realism or social constructionism', *Organization*, **7**(3): 531–5.

Van Maanen, J. (1988), *Tales of the Field: On Writing Ethnography*, London, UK and Chicago, US: University of Chicago Press.

Warren, L. (2004) 'Negotiating entrepreneurial identity: communities of practice and changing discourses', *International Journal of Entrepreneurship and Innovation*, **5**(1): 25–35.

Watson, T.J. (1994), *In Search of Management: Culture Chaos and Control in Managerial Work*, London, UK and New York, US: Routledge.

Watson, T.J. (1995), 'Rhetoric, discourse and argument in organizational sense making: a reflexive tale', *Organizational Studies*, **16**(5): 805–21.

Watson, T.J. (1996), 'How do managers think? Identity, morality and pragmatism in managerial theory and practice', *Management Learning*, **27**(3): 323–41.

Watson, T.J. (1997), 'Theorizing managerial work: a pragmatic pluralist approach to interdisciplinary research', *British Journal of Management*, **8**(1): 3–8.

Watson, T.J. (2000), 'Ethnographic fiction science: making sense of managerial work and organisational research processes with Caroline and Terry', *Organization*, **7**(3): 489–510.

Watson, T.J. (2004), 'Managers, managism and the tower of babble: making sense of managerial pseudo-jargon', *International Journal for the Sociology of Language*, **166**: 67–82.

Weiner, E.S.C. and Simpson, J.A. (eds) (prep.) (1989), *The Oxford English Dictionary* (second edition), Oxford: Clarendon Press.

Wenger, E. (1998), *Communities of Practice: Learning, Meaning and Identity*, Cambridge, UK and New York, US: Cambridge University Press.

Wilson, C. (1978), *The Outsider*, London: Picador.

Zerubavel, E. (1981), *Hidden Rhythms: Schedules and Calendars in Social Life*, Berkeley: University of California Press.

Zijderveld, A.C. (1979), *On Clichés: The Supersedure of Meaning by Function in Modernity*, London: Routledge and Kegan Paul.

Zimmer, C. and Aldrich, H. (1987), 'Resource mobilization through ethnic networks: kinship and friendship ties of shopkeepers in England', *Sociological Perspectives*, **30**(4): 422–45.

Index